Unfolding
Journey

A Story of Self Discovery

Unfolding Journey

Spiritual Principles

to Assist

in Connecting to Spirit

and Being

Your Authentic Self

Sharon Gardner

Unfolding Journey
Copyright © 2001 by Sharon Gardner

Published and distributed by Gardner Publishing
493 Scenic Dr. Santa Barbara, CA 93103
(805) 969-3822

Edited by Eileen Conrad

Cover and book design by Frazier Graphic Design,
Santa Barbara, CA

Printed in the United States of America

This book is dedicated

to those seeking

to know themselves,

to those who want to live their life

with purpose,

and to those who are grateful

for the journey.

ACKNOWLEDGMENTS

Thank you God for giving me the opportunities to grow and the resources to help me. Thank you for repeating the messages in ways I could hear. Thank you for giving me faith and teaching me to trust.

I offer my thanks and gratitude to the following:

My loving husband, Joe Frazier, for the support you give and for the book and graphic designs you created.

Eileen Conrad for editing, organizational input and giving me spiritual support.

Roger Leadbetter for print consultation.

Mary Quinn, English professor, for the initial book review, organization and helping me to understand the process.

Bill Richardson, my first writing teacher, who helped me to believe I could write.

Alan Cohen, author, for encouraging me to write my story and share my wisdom.

Julie Newendorp, my dear friend and associate for seeing me through this process of growth, holding my hand and reminding me who I am.

All my clients and students who have encouraged me to write what I teach, given me inspiration and received what I have to give.

My dear friends who a have held the vision with me, Cathy and Tim Thompson, Sara Patton, Nancy Coburn, Gail Saunders and Joanna Lindegaard. To all my friends and who have given encouragement to me and to those writers who have inspired and shown me the steps to take.

Unfolding Journey

Spiritual Principles to Assist You in Connecting
to Spirit and Being Your Authentic Self

Sharon Gardner

CONTENTS

FOREWORD
by Alan Cohen

Wherever I go I meet people hungering and thirsting for more meaning and purpose in their lives. "Who am I?" and "What am I supposed to be doing with my life?" are the two questions—really quests—that so many people are asking, overtly or below the surface of their external pursuits. In a culture where so much emphasis is placed upon material success, our deep need for spiritual fulfillment is powerfully magnified.

When someone comes along who can assist us to find the answers to our personal quest, it is a great blessing indeed. What a gift to meet someone who can guide us to the fulfillment of our own dreams! Such a one deserves our immediate and focused attention.

Sharon Gardner is such a guide. Sharon is a powerful teacher because she is for real. She has experienced both earthly hardships and heady joy; she has worked her way through physical and emotional pain and made sense of them as stepping stones on her journey. Sharon has looked herself in the mirror on a regular basis and striven to match her actions with her values; she has learned to love herself and carve out a relationship and career in harmony with her heart's desires. She has learned to walk her own path without apology.

When I first met Sharon over 12 years ago, I felt that I had been reunited with a soul sister. She had that look in her eyes, as if to say, "I know you!" She did. Since that time we have become good friends and seen each other through many of life's challenges and celebrations. During all of that time, I have found Sharon to be a woman of the highest integrity. She is dedicated to truth and spiritual service.

When I was going through a painful experience I went to Sharon as a counselor and healer. In my vulnerable state, I shared my heart's aching with her, and called out to the universe for support, through her. And she was there. She was really there. I felt unconditionally loved and supported, and empowered to move beyond my fears and self-imposed judgments. Intuitively Sharon found the place in me that was calling for nurturing, and gave it. I walked out of our session feeling renewed and healed. I have since consulted with Sharon on a number of occasions, and have always felt validated.

I have also invited Sharon to teach seminars with me, and our participants have issued glowing reports of the remarkable transformations they have experienced through their work together.

Now Sharon has recorded her story and her wisdom. This book is a gift. *Unfolding Journey* contains all the elements of the spiritual path that you are likely to encounter, artfully illuminated by one who has learned to tread that path with dignity and love. Sharon pulls no punches in describing the difficulties she has encountered, nor does she compromise in declaring the spiritual truths she has discovered. This book is both lofty and grounded, a perfect syllabus for integrated learning.

What I like most about *Unfolding Journey* is that it is practical. This teaching is for people who want to make spiritual sense out of their earthly journey. It is about health, relationships, love, money, family and all of the things you so ardently want to make work for you. If you study these principles and put them into action, I promise your life will change in the most wonderful way.

One more note: Sharon Gardner is an impeccable model of a woman in her own power. I meet so many women (and men) who have given their power away to their spouse, family, work, or society and then forget who they are. Much of the spiritual work of women in our culture is to reclaim their ability to live their own life rather than the life others would ask of them. Sharon maintains a beautiful synthesis of her feminine and masculine energies and weaves them into an excellent model for both women and men. Practicing the principles in this book will surely assist you to do the same.

My deepest thanks to Sharon for recording her wisdom, and to you for discovering your own.

Alan Cohen

INTRODUCTION

The *Spiritual Principles and Practices* presented in this book have assisted me on my **unfolding journey to know and become my authentic self** (being real, genuine in expressing true feelings, being true to myself and what is right for me). They are offered to assist you in connecting with Spirit and your authentic self. The *Spiritual Principles* will guide you to live your life with awareness, compassion, self-acceptance and choice. The *Spiritual Practices* will show you how to do it. All the answers are within you. Learn to connect with your Spirit, listen and trust.

Use and apply these *Spiritual Principles and Practices* to assist in your process of self-discovery, self-acceptance and empowerment. Learn how to let go of past guilt, shame, anger, and sadness. Release limiting beliefs and patterns of behavior that were programmed into you by your family, culture and religion. **"Your history is not your destiny,"** says Alan Cohen, a spiritual self-development lecturer and best-selling author of *The Dragon Doesn't Live Here Anymore.*

You can change and transform your life and realize you have choice. **Choice empowers you** to create yourself and your life anew. It is the power of love within you that allows you to change and be genuine in your interactions with others. The power of love enables you to stop reacting out of fear. Love allows you to forgive and accept yourself and others. Learn to connect to the love within you.   This book will assist you in loving and accepting yourself. It teaches you to **listen and trust** Spirit and **claim your wisdom and power**. It will help you embrace your Soul's journey and know its purpose. Live your life authentically!

My Path

I began exploring metaphysics (the unseen realm beyond the physical) when I was nineteen by practicing yoga and meditation to handle the pain of migraine headaches. The medication the doctors prescribed did not prevent the headaches or stop the pain. Through meditation and relaxation, I was able to lessen their intensity and manage the pain. Yoga led me to further study eastern religions, astrology, palmistry, numerology, past lives, esotericism and cosmology.

My education includes a BS in social work and psychology with master's level work in counseling psychology and numerous workshops in self-awareness and self-actualization. During my twenties and early thirties, all of this knowledge was satisfying my intellect and answering questions that my Baptist upbringing did not answer.

A near-death experience in 1983 (more on that later) opened me up to life. It was an awakening of my Spiritual

Self, and the beginning of the process of living my life authentically. I began an intense study of the healing arts including Therapeutic Touch, Reiki, Reflexology, Grof breath work, re-birthing, and the use of visualization and imagery to access the transpersonal self. I studied with spiritual healers, psychics, shamans, and kahunas. My exploration included the New Thought religions of Unity Church, Church of Religious Science and the Course in Miracles. Deepak Chopra's writings were also a major influence.

An important mentor for me is Alan Cohen. I began working with him as "healer in residence" and co-facilitator at spiritual retreats in Hawaii. Working with him helped me develop confidence to lead my own retreats. He also has given me the support to write and share what I know. The *Spiritual Principles* presented are some of the principles created and taught by Alan Cohen and myself, and are based on metaphysical universal principles that are also taught in New Thought religion.

Many times following Spirit along this unfolding journey, I felt as if I was leaping off a cliff hoping a net would catch me. I have found myself blindly walking up a mountain not knowing what lay around the next bend, having lost sight of the top and why I chose this path. Unsure of my steps I walked on the edge of a precipice trying to keep my eyes straight ahead, not looking back or down. Breathing through the fear of the unknown, and asking, "Is this my life's path?"

Now, my understanding of spiritual truths is real for me experientially, emotionally and spiritually. Before the near-death experience, I had learned them intellectually, but did not know it in my heart or my being. My healing path, the process of letting go of guilt, shame, sadness, fear and learning to accept and love my self, began when I understood why I was alive. I discovered I had a purpose for being here.

I am a Life Choices counselor,teacher, Therapeutic Touch (see Appendix) and Reiki healing practitioner (energy worker). Since 1986, I have worked with groups and individuals practicing and teaching Therapeutic Touch healing, meditation and the principles of love, compassion, self-acceptance and non-judgement. I have learned how to listen to Spirit, and have taught others to listen to their Inner Source (Spirit), to trust the information and guidance, and to act upon it by living in alignment with their Soul's Purpose.

The Challenge

One day while I was meditating and listening to Spirit, I received a message. *Write. Write. Write.* I did not want to believe or trust the message. Writing was the next step in my growth process, and it brought up fear, doubt and confusion. Was I willing to accept this challenging assignment, this "calling?"

Spirit is always challenging us to move beyond our comfort zone and to grow to achieve our full potential. Most times we do not even have a clue what we are here to do or how we are to go about it. I wanted to know how I was to do this assignment. Listening to the guidance of Spirit shows us the way and the how.

I had to discern that the guidance I had been receiving was, in fact, coming from Spirit, not the voice of my clients asking me to write what I was teaching, or the voice that said I could not do it. I had to learn to trust and release the fear of becoming more visible, as well as old fears of being burned at the stake, exiled or abused. I had to release thoughts that I was not good enough, did not have the talent or skill to write a book. Being afraid is not a good excuse to not follow the guidance of Spirit. I had to feel the fear, not let it stop me, and do it anyway.

I have been in the practice of listening to Spirit since the big wake-up call of my near-death experience. At that time, I received my first "calling." A clear message from God heard as my Inner Voice to do the healing work I am currently doing. I have had to trust Spirit in many instances when I did not know what lay ahead or how I was to move ahead.

Being in integrity, taking action that is consistent with what I feel is best or right, means everything to me. Trusting is imperative. It had to learn to Honor My Spirit by listening, trusting and taking action. The guidance was to write this book.

The *Spiritual Principles and Practices* that follow support the process of self-discovery and will assist you in living your life's purpose from your authentic self with ease and joy. They are: being grounded and centered, setting intention, having trust, compassion, love, forgiveness, non-judgment, non-attachment, and being in integrity. These *Spiritual Principles and Practices* are at the heart of what I have learned, and I am still applying and practicing them as I continue to grow on my unfolding journey.

WHY AM I ALIVE ?

"There are no mistakes, no coincidences.
All events are blessings
given to us to learn from."
Elisabeth Kubler-Ross

Waking up from the anesthesia, I was again aware of pain. What had happened? My doctor, a gynecologist and an expert in infertility, was bending over me holding my hand. There were tears in his eyes. He said, "We saved you." I remember thinking, saved me from what and for what? He explained, "We had to cut you open to stop the internal bleeding. You'll be fine now."

I had a near-death experience and was alive again. A wave of sadness washed over me. I did not want to be saved. I did not want to be alive. I wanted to be in peace. Why was I still alive?

The doctors were amazed by my condition and what caused the bleeding. It was a rare occurrence. As they gave their various explanations, I kept remembering the peace I had felt when my spirit had left my body. I did not want to be alive again. There was too much pain in my life both physically and emotionally!

The memory of what I had just experienced hit me like a tidal wave. A month before in April 1983, I had undergone surgery to remove a fertilized egg that had not made it into my womb and was growing in my abdominal cavity. It was my second ectopic pregnancy. The first had been in 1981, when I lost my left fallopian tube and the embryo due to a tubule pregnancy (where the embryo grows in the tube). The first time I found out I was pregnant I was so surprised. I was 32 years old and married to my third husband. I had thought I could not get pregnant because of scarring in my fallopian tubes due to repeated occurrences of pelvic inflammatory disease (PID).

In my early twenties I had an inter-uterine device (IUD) implanted in my uterus to prevent pregnancy. The IUD caused the PID and subsequent scarring. Later, I realized that the problems with my female reproductive organs (pelvic infections, vaginal yeast infections, and infertility) were emotionally connected to the sexual guilt and shame I stored in my body. My sixteen-year-old male baby-sitter had sexually molested me when I was eight years old. I never talked about it. Having been raised as a Baptist, my religion prohibited sex outside of marriage. This contributed to the guilt and shame I felt not only as a child being sexual, but later as a young unmarried adult exploring sex.

The surprise and loss of the pregnancy, both occurring the same day within minutes of each other, sent me into a downward emotional spiral. One minute the doctor was saying, "You are pregnant," then after doing an ultrasound to determine the placement of the baby, he said, "The tube is bursting and we need to do surgery now to remove it"

There was tremendous feeling of elation that I was pregnant and deep loss that I could not carry the baby. I was intensely afraid of going through surgery and losing the fallopian tube.

Trying to relieve my fears, my doctor told me, "There is good news! You will be able to conceive again even though you are losing one tube. I can repair the blocked tube by performing microsurgery on it. I feel strongly I can open it, and you will have a good chance of conceiving again." It was going to be worth going through all this! My fears assuaged, I placed myself in his hands.

With great hope, I tried for a year and a half to become pregnant after the surgery. However, as I focused on conceiving, I never let myself grieve the child I lost. Each month I experienced anticipation and grief at the sight of my monthly flow. My tears would flow as the blood flowed from me.

I took my temperature every morning before rising to determine when I was ovulating. I would make a date for sex with my husband. Trying to have sex to make a baby at prearranged times never seemed to work. Inevitably, we would have a fight, or he would work late and be too tired for sex. Often it was so strained between us, sex, let alone lovemaking, did not occur. We just could not seem to get together. It was so frustrating. Our communication was not good. We did not know how to get close. The marriage was not going well, but then it had not from the beginning.

I found out that my 6'3" handsome, athletic husband was having affairs. He was a charismatic man. Women and men liked him and found him attractive. I did, too. It made me feel good to think I had him when so many others seemed to want him, but I never really had him. He could not commit to our marriage or to me. This was my third husband, and I was not willing to give up the marriage. I had to make it work, yet I did not know how to have a healthy, successful marriage. I was committed to do all I could do by trying to please him and being what he wanted me to be.

He denied the affairs. I denied that I felt something was going on or even knew. I had forgiven him for the first affair that occurred during the second year of our marriage. He only admitted to having this affair because I caught him. I wanted us to be together so much that I was willing to overlook it. I thought a baby would bring us together, a misperception many women have. It was a difficult time for me because I continually denied my feelings and intuitions.

After a year and a half, I gave up trying to get pregnant or even trying to have sex with my husband when I was ovulating. I could not handle the rejection. I felt unattractive and unlovable. I sought solace outside my marriage by having an affair too. I reacted because I was feeling lonely, frustrated, and hopeless. In the back of my mind, I sought revenge! I wanted to get back at my husband. Yet, I kept the affair a secret because I was afraid of losing him.

One day, I had the feeling that something was different inside me. I felt pregnant again! I was hopeful and scared. I was afraid that the embryo would not be in the right place, it was not my husband's baby, and I felt guilty for getting pregnant.

What was I going to do? I prayed that somehow it was not true. If it was true, I was afraid I would lose this baby, too. I could not face telling my husband I was pregnant, and that it was not his baby. Deep inside I felt guilty for what I had done, and ashamed for having judged him for having affairs. I was no better than he, even though I self-righteously clung to the belief that I was justified. It took me a long time to face the truth of my own behavior and to forgive myself.

I confided my secret to only one person. I told my ex-sister-in-law who is like a sister to me. I felt she was someone that could understand me. She did. She loved me and never judged me. I felt safe in telling her my secret about the affair and resulting pregnancy. She listened and told me the truth would probably come out if I had this child. I did not want to face that.

In silence, I waited until enough time passed to take the in-home pregnancy test. I was pregnant. One afternoon a few weeks later, I felt a familiar pain in my lower right abdomen. I had begun spotting. I cried as I made my way to the hospital. An ultrasound test confirmed my greatest fear. Another surgery was required to remove the embryo that had not even made it into the tube leading to the womb. It was attempting to grow its fragile life in my abdominal cavity.

As I lay in the hospital awaiting my fate, I heard the damning voice of my father inside my head judging me, labeling me an adulteress. I couldn't breathe as guilt and shame smothered me like a heavy blanket. What would my father think of me now if he knew I had gotten pregnant by a man other than my husband?

As I waited in the hospital emergency room with severe pain in my right side, fear shot through me like a cold rod of steel impaling me to a wall. I couldn't move. I was going to lose this baby, too, and all possibility of having children. I so wanted a baby, yet I did not want one in this situation. As I faced another surgery, I felt God was punishing me for what I had done. I thought this was the best thing that could ever happen. Now my husband would never know.

However, the punishment of losing the baby and not being able to conceive did not absolve the guilt. I felt even more guilt and shame. I held it all inside. I kept the secret inside my body and my heart. The emotional pain was too deep. I stuffed the tears and stopped crying because I was afraid of tearing apart the stitches from the surgery. I went numb.

The Awakening

I had really wanted a baby, yet felt I did not deserve the one I had just lost. I was not recovering from the surgery either physically or emotionally. I was bleeding internally, without a clue to what was going on inside of me. I only knew I did not feel well, and was not getting my strength back.

The day I was taken to the hospital emergency room I felt excruciating abdominal, chest and arm pain. I had difficulty breathing. I could not stand up. My blood pressure was dropping. In the emergency room, I told my husband to call my mother as I lay dying. He left to call. I remember being alone in the pain and fear...waiting...

Then, the pain stopped. I felt relaxed, floating in a bright light with no sense of self. I was light. I experienced such a state of peace and a sense of well being. I felt loved as I was bathed and drawn deeper into the light. The peace was beyond description. There was no sense of the physical, no body weight, no separate self. There was no pain or heaviness, only lightness and a deep expansive feeling of love.

The next thing I remembered after the experience of peace and love was waking up in pain! I do not know how long I experienced this extraordinary state. I never asked my doctors. We never talked about my near-death experience. It was the early 80's, and I did not fully accept the experience or discuss it with anyone for several years. The near-death experience was the beginning of my spiritual awakening after being shut down emotionally and spiritually for so many years.

Later, alone lying in the hospital bed, the realization that I could not have children hit me slowly, then picked up momentum. I began sobbing softly, then a rush of tears as the breath caught in gasps. The sobs came from deep within the core of my body and soul. I felt as if I would break apart. The intensity increased, and I wanted the pain to stop. I did not want to be on this journey. I cried out to God, "This can't be my life! Why didn't I stay dead? Why am I alive?"

MY SEARCH FOR IDENTITY

"God is in the sadness and the laughter,
in the bitter and the sweet.
There is a divine purpose behind everything — and
therefore a divine presence in everything."
Neale Donald Walsch

As a child, I forgot I was a spiritual being having a human experience. I over-identified with the experiences and feelings of being human. I forgot who I was. Forgetting is common among humans. We have forgotten that we truly are spiritual beings.

The human experience I had as a child was very confusing. I was the second child born into an interracial family in 1949. Being different is challenging for anybody, whether the difference is because of size, color, race, disability, religion, culture, intelligence or economics. It seems our greatest challenge as human beings is to accept our selves and each other. There is such diversity in our country, in the world, and in nature. Why is it so hard for humans to accept differences? As a child it certainly was hard for me to accept that I was different.

I am racially mixed with African American, Native American and Caucasian heritage. My father has wavy hair, light brown skin, and is an African American mixed with Native American and Caucasian ancestry. My Caucasian mother is very white with freckled skin and straight, light brown hair. My coloring is honey colored tan when I am out in the sun, otherwise I am olive skinned with curly brown hair that was considered "good hair" by color-struck black folks who felt that kinky hair was not acceptable.

The prevailing belief was that the lighter you were the better you were. The whiter you were made you more acceptable to both blacks and whites. Yet at the same time, being looked down upon by blacks and whites as being uppity or "trying to be better than." You were discriminated against simply because you were light. Hence, lighter skinned "black folks" tended to stay together and be more exclusive. Mixed race "colored folks" had to find their way and place.

Since slavery, blacks have been considered inferior, less than human. The lessons of separateness and privilege were well learned by Negroes from the "white slave master." The message was that no matter how light your skin, you still weren't good enough. I internalized and believed the messages from this cultural conditioning.

I did not know who I was racially until I was in my twenties. Generally, I experienced non-acceptance though some blacks accepted me as black and some whites accepted me as racially mixed or thought I was white. Most of the time I felt as if I did not fit in with any race or group. I felt isolated and invisible. I was like a chameleon changing to fit in with whomever I was interacting. I struggled with my identity.

In St. Paul, Minnesota, there were not many mixed-race people. My parents, who married in the mid-forties, were unusual. There were not many interracial couples. I did not grow up with other kids like myself or see other interracial couples until later in life. My birth certificate proclaimed my legal identity as Negro (if you had 1/16 Negro blood you were considered Negro). I have been called Negro, mulatto, colored, "yellow nigger," bright (because I was so light-skinned), black, and now African American. I prefer racially mixed.

I am often mistaken for anything other than African-American. People think I am Caucasian, Native American, Greek, Puerto Rican, Creole, Hawaiian, Spanish, or of Jewish ethnicity. Growing up, I felt pulled between being either black or white. Did I have to choose? I did not know which race to identify with since I did not want to reject any part of my heritage. Legally, I could not be racially mixed.

I had no confidence in myself. I felt nothing but confusion as I looked to others to define me. I had little self-esteem growing up. Not only was I confused over my racial identity, I felt awkward and different because of my size. I am six feet tall, but even as a child in kindergarten; I was a head taller than my classmates. To make it worse, my father, who is a Baptist minister, taught me that I was born sinful and unworthy of God's love. What was I to do but try to be good and please my father, God and, of course, others?

I lost the innocence of my childhood at eight-years-old. Several events happened. My younger brother was born. My mother was emotionally unstable, and I took over many of her household responsibilities including helping her with my younger brother. At times, a teenage boy, who was a member of our church, would help out by taking care of us. I was sexually molested when I was entrusted into his care. It occurred many times, and I never told my parents. I thought it was my fault for being too cute. I knew being sexual was sinful. I felt ashamed.

My heart shut down from the overwhelming pain and confusion. I did not know how to handle the feelings. I did not speak about this experience until my mid-thirties when the memories returned. The molestation set in motion many unhealthy behavioral patterns that took years to change.

The only place I felt peace was in nature. Luckily, every summer, I went to a religious camp on Snail Lake that was near my home. Swimming in the cool clear water, horseback riding and hiking in the woods gave me comfort. The strength of the earth beneath me was calming as I sat cradled among the tall oak trees. I continued going to camp through high school.

During my junior year in high school, I had my first experience of God in Colorado's Rocky Mountains at a ranch operated by a non-denominational Christian organization. I began to see that God was more than the judgmental, punishing God of the religion of my youth. I realized that God is a universal creative force present in everything. I saw God in the trees, the flowers, the running stream, and in the mountains. "Could it mean God was in me too?"

In the mountains of Colorado, at sixteen, my heart began to open again. Mostly, I experienced this out in nature. When I was with people, my heart would shut down again. I would lose myself with people and would focus on pleasing them to feel loved and accepted.

As a child, I was very intuitive. I felt other people's emotions and could not separate mine from theirs. There was a lot of emotional upheaval in our family because my mother and father could not accept their racial differences. I was always in the middle of their disagreements because I assumed the role of mediator and tried to create harmony in the family. I did not know what to do with all of their feelings. My parents called me "overly sensitive." Family conflicts made me sick with bronchitis, sore throats, and migraine headaches.

Being intuitive, I would know things, such as who was

calling or coming by the house. I even saw "things" as a young child. I saw the spirits of those members of our church who had died. I saw and talked to angels and Jesus. When I was three, I remember Jesus and two angels standing at the foot of my bed speaking to me just before I fell asleep. The next morning I told my father and he said, "You have to wait 'til you die to see Jesus. You have to accept Jesus as your savior to go to heaven and see him." I loved Jesus and the angels that visited me. My father did not believe my experiences with Jesus so I did as he instructed and accepted Jesus as my savior. I wanted Jesus to stay with me, and I did not want to wait until I died.

I kept having unusual experiences until I was eight when an epileptic boy from our church died from a seizure. He had befriended me, and when he died his spirit came to say good-bye. When I told my father he got scared and told me it was the devil's work. It seemed the devil was always doing things that upset my father. So, I told Jesus I did not want to see things anymore. It all stopped. I did not see spirits, angels or Jesus anymore, even though at times I would "feel or sense" their presence around me.

Shortly after telling Jesus I did not want to see things, I accidentally ran into a boy on the playground and bumped heads. One of my eyes was swollen shut, and both eyes were black and blue for a long time. The eye doctor told me there was not any permanent damage, but

discovered that I was nearsighted. I had to get glasses to
see after that. I shut down both emotionally and
intuitively when I was eight. It was a very traumatic year.
It was not until my mid-thirties that my inner vision
returned.

The search for myself began that summer in the
mountains and was reading a book about reincarnation. I
felt there was truth in the experiences of the young woman
who had been hypnotized and regressed to a past life. I
again put my interests on the back burner, as they did not
fit into my religion. I did not begin the exploration of my
spirituality, my true identity again until age nineteen.

My awareness of my identity came not only from my
metaphysical studies, but also from psychology, which was
my major in college. As humans we are more than the
identification of our race, religion, or gender. We are more
that the role we play as husband, wife, mother, daughter,
worker, therapist, hiker, or sport enthusiast. We are not
our job, bank account, beliefs, emotions or even our body.
These roles and identities can change.

We are all spiritual beings having experiences of being
in a body with emotions, beliefs and thoughts that come
and go, and relationships and roles that change. It is up to
us to discover our true essence—our identity. To know
who thinks the thought—the part of us that is aware that
we exist.

In my search for my identity, the many wounds from
my childhood and the deep programming of believing and

feeling worthless had to be overcome. It was through my healing process that I was learning to know and accept myself. It took me a long time to realize that God is within me, and is not a condemning force outside of me. This realization did not occur until my near-death experience at age thirty-four.

Once I began to understand that I am a spirit in a body having these experiences to learn who I truly am, I began releasing the over-identification with the wounds and the roles. I was not just a racially mixed child, who had been molested at eight years old, or the sexually guilty, shameful person who was a people pleaser, or the woman who was divorced three times because she did not know how to have a healthy relationship. I discovered there was more to me than the wounds, and I found myself on a path of self-discovery and self-acceptance using these life lessons to grow.

I am on a path to know myself, to be aware of myself beyond the limiting beliefs and the identification with roles and concerns of being one race or another. My path has had many ups and downs, starts and stops. Many times I lost my way, lost faith, and fell into darkness. The fear, guilt and shame mired me down and I felt worthlessness many times. Fear would stop me from creating what I wanted.

Sometimes, we think of our personal and spiritual growth as a straight line. However, we grow more like a spiral. When we are on the down side of the spiral we think we are backsliding or failing, although the doubt and fear can help us be aware of what no longer works. They give us direction. If what you are doing does not feel right or causes you to feel pain, stop and go another way or do something different. At those times when we experience tremendous growth we are on the up side of the spiral. Notice that you are further along your path now than you were a year ago or five years ago. You are spiraling in your growth.

You are always on your path of growth, for once begun there in no turning back. Even if you think you are not on the path, you are! Author Marianne Williamson says, "The spiritual path...is simply the journey of living our lives. Everyone is on a spiritual path; most people just don't know it." Spirit is using everything you experience as lessons for your growth and evolvement.

⟿SPIRITUAL PRINCIPLE⟿
Everything Serves.

"There is no part of life that does not contain lessons. If you are alive, there are lessons to be learned." Says author Cherie Carter-Scott.

As my inner vision came back, I was able to see the experiences, the false beliefs, the shame and guilt and see that it was not who I truly was. The pain was not my essence it was only an experience, a human experience. All I had gone through and experienced was exactly what I needed to learn in order to grow.

The Story of "The Butterfly"

One day a small opening appeared on a cocoon. A man sat and watched for the butterfly for several hours as it struggled to force its body through that little hole. Then, it seemed to stop making any progress. It appeared as it had gotten as far as it could and it could go no further. So, the man decided to help the butterfly. He took a pair of scissors and snipped off the remaining bit of the cocoon. The butterfly then emerged easily, but it had a swollen body and small, shriveled wings.

The man continued to watch the butterfly because he expected that, at any moment, the wings would enlarge and expand to be able to support the body, which would contract in time. Neither happened! In fact, the butterfly spent the rest of its life crawling around with a swollen body and shriveled wings. It never was able to fly.

What the man in his kindness and haste did not understand was that the restricting cocoon and the struggle required for the butterfly to get through the tiny opening were God's way of forcing fluid from the body of the butterfly into its wings. Then, it would be ready for flight once it achieved its freedom from the cocoon.

Sometimes, struggles are exactly what we need in our life. If God allowed us to go through life without any obstacles, it would cripple us. We would not be as strong as we could have been. We could never soar. Be thankful for the challenges. They strengthen you.

DISCOVERING WHO YOU ARE

"I have lived on the lip of insanity,
wanting to know reasons, knocking on a door.
It opens.
I've been knocking from the inside."
Rumi

Who Am I?

The spiritual path is a quest to discover your true self. This quest takes many forms and usually begins with the question, "Who am I?" This question is asked repeatedly by those who have discovered a level of personal awareness as they release patterns of behavior and beliefs that have defined them which no longer support their true self. Asking this question leads us to discover and be our true self, the authentic self...living and being the essence of our Soul, living from our Spirit.

To know oneself becomes the path, the unfolding journey. "Who am I?" "Why am I here?" "What is my life's purpose?" are at the heart of the spiritual quest.

Like so many others, finding the answers became my quest. The answers received helped me come to terms with my identity. It was through the spiritual path and the *Spiritual Principle and Practices* that follow that I came to know and accept myself and recognize that I am valuable and lovable.

⤳SPIRITUAL PRINCIPLE⤳
*You are a Spiritual Being having
a Human Experience.*

You are a spiritual being filled with extraordinary qualities. Your Spirit is part of the creative energy of the whole universe in which everything is connected. You are wisdom. You are creative. You are peace. You are joy. You are strength. You are compassion. You are love. You are a creative being and you are continually creating your life. Your essence is love from which all else pours forth. When you are centered in your essence, you are connected to who you are, and you are connected to the love that you are.

Experiences connecting you to your true self can open you to the realization that God, Spirit, Inner Source is within and around you in all things. Experiences that connect you to your authentic self are: meditation and prayer; being in nature ... watching a sunset, walking on the beach or in the woods; being with something or someone you love; being creative, etc.

The spiritual path is a process of clearing away everything that is not you, clearing away the blocks to love. It is as if you have on many layers of clothing and you see only the clothing, the outer garments and think, "This piece of clothing is me." As you take off a piece of clothing, you discover that there is yet another layer of clothing and another. These layer are not the real you. In fact, these layers are covering the essence, the magnificent light that you are as a spiritual being.

The Spiritual Self

What is the Spiritual Self? Our Spiritual Self is one with God, The Creative Life Force. Our Spiritual Self is love, The Divine Essence that knows all and is all. Our Souls are the individualized expressed creative energy that is one with God. There is no separation. We are comprised of Spirit, Soul, mind, emotions and body.

You may call that power that is greater than your ego, mind, personality self: Spirit, Inner Source, God, Great Spirit, All That Is, Inner Wisdom, Intuitive Self, Spiritual Self, Higher Power, Higher Self, The Universe, Universal

Mind. Use whatever term works best for you. I use the terms interchangeably.

God (Spirit) is within us and around us and in all things. You cannot separate yourself from the whole. You are from God and a part of God, a part of the whole. You are whole. You have everything you need within yourself. You are Divine!

~SPIRITUAL PRINCIPLE~
You are One with God.

You are only separate if you think you are. We have been conditioned by society and some religions to think that we are separate from God. We are in separate bodies so we must be separate. We believe we are separate from each other and God. Our thoughts of fear or judgment separate us from each other and from our true self, our Divine self. Our thoughts create separation. It is only a thought. We have many thoughts that are not true. For example, the thought that you are unworthy or not good enough is not true, yet many people believe it..

From a seed a tree grows limbs, leaves, and bears fruit that also has seeds. They are all part of the tree, the whole. Does a limb or a piece of fruit view themselves as separate from the tree? No. They are all part of the tree with their own individual expression and function. When the fruit falls from the tree or the seed separates from the fruit, it may choose to see itself as separate and no longer a part of the tree. Taking the analogy another step, the fruit or seed could imagine that there was something wrong with them and that is why they were separated from the tree. In fact, many of us tend to think that we are separate from God because of something we did, because we are bad, evil or sinful. We may think that we are not a part of God, not part of the whole.

It is not true that you are separate from God. You are one with God. You have only lost the connection by perceiving that the connection is no longer there. It is only a misperception that the connection is gone. You need only focus your attention on the connection and it is there. Do whatever helps you to perceive your connection, like following your breath, meditating, or taking a walk in nature.

Breathing Exercise

Take a few deep breaths. Focus your attention on the breath as it moves through your nostrils. Feel the breath as it moves down the back of your throat, moving into and filling your chest and abdomen. Feel the breath as it moves out. Allow the breath to move as you observe the breath moving. Be aware of any thoughts that arise in your mind. Be aware of any feelings. Be aware of any sensations or pain in your body. Be aware. Watch your internal process. Allow your attention to return to your breath. Be with yourself by focusing on your breath.

Connection

We are Spirit, Soul, mind, emotional body and physical body. You are a whole Divine being. You are more than your parts. The parts are connected and interpenetrate each other. They cannot be separated. Each influences the other. Our mind influences both our emotions and our body. Our body influences our thoughts and emotions. Our Soul influences the mind. Our Spirit influences all aspects of ourselves. At times, it is a two way street. Other times, it is a five way street. We may not know if we are coming or going because we feel so many influences. It is important to focus on our connection with Spirit instead of separation.

The Soul

Our Soul (the seed) is the Divine individualized expression of God. It is that part of us that continues through and beyond time to experience life in many forms. Our Soul may carry emotional pain from experiences by holding onto limiting beliefs and misperceptions. Our Soul also knows what it needs to experience in this life to grow and evolve and remember its connection to Source. The Soul may need healing. The Soul may need conscious reconnection with Source due to some trauma or misperception that it was separated or abandoned by God. God the Source communicates the truth of our being to us through our intuition, inner hearing, inner sight, gut feeling, and knowing, even though we may not know how we know. To know one's Soul is to know one's true self.

The Mind

The mind is like software that has information. It communicates through the brain, the hardware. The mind contains and accesses information from Spirit, our Soul, intellectual scientific learning, and experiential learning. It operates in critical linear thinking. The mind also accesses Universal mind or consciousness (the ability to tap into what is happening with others, the earth, and the cosmos). An example of this occurs when scientists in different parts of the world simultaneously have the same idea, theory or solution.

The mind brings the information into us, either through the emotional body or the physical body in a form we can use. We are the "thinker" using the mind to create with our thoughts and emotions.

The Emotional and Physical Body

The emotional body contains all our feelings, including love, happiness, joy, contentment, peace, sadness, fear, anxiety, confusion, anger, grief, and shame. The emotional body feels. It does not process by thinking. The physical body processes everything we experience and sometimes holds onto what we experience. The physical body is the vehicle for our expression and our experience of the physical world. The emotions need to move through the physical body like a river flowing into the ocean. Emotions need the breath to move. If we do not breathe when experiencing our feelings, they get stuck in the body. Most of us hold our breath when we are scared or hurt. We need only to breathe to keep clear emotionally.

When we hold onto emotions and think thoughts that scare or hurt us our physical body goes out of balance. The natural state of our physical body is one of balance and harmony. Life is constantly challenging us to stay in balance and harmony with many aspects of our being— Spirit, soul, mind, emotions and body.

BEING GROUNDED

"We simply cannot be effective in daily life
...or attempt to fulfill life's
purpose if we are not grounded."
Cyndi Dale

Because you are Spirit in a body, it is essential that you be grounded to exist on the Earth plane, to be present, and to handle the affairs of your life.

Do you need to be more present and focused on what you are doing, or whom you are with? Do you feel scattered, spaced out, disorganized or confused? Do you bump into things, feel out of balance, out of your body or only in your head? You may need to get grounded.

Being Grounded

Being grounded is the process of connecting to your body and to the Earth. You are a spiritual being in a body on the Earth having an experience of being human. In order to be fully yourself, you need to connect to your body and be fully in your body which enables you to connect to the world around you. You have a tremendous amount of spiritual energy of love, compassion, wisdom, creativity, and joy. You also have a lot of mental energy, emotional energy and physical energy.

An electrical circuit needs to be grounded to allow the energy to flow and illuminate a light bulb. If the light bulb were not grounded, it would burst, blowing the circuit. We are similar. All of our spiritual, mental, emotional, and physical energy needs to be grounded so that we do not feel crazy or scattered and out of control. You have a tremendous amount of energy that needs to be grounded so that you can use it.

Benefits of Being Grounded

- You are able to focus and be present with what is going on in the moment.

- You have a sense of being connected to your body and a sense of strength and stability.

- You are able to handle the affairs of your daily life with ease.

- You can show up for appointments on time, feel organized and in control.

- You can allow the emotional energy to flow through you, and not get blown away by other people's emotions.

- You can handle the emotional, physical, mental (your thoughts and beliefs) and the magnificent powerful spiritual energy that you are.

Why People Are Not Grounded

1. Physical pain can cause us to be ungrounded. If there is pain in the body, you may not want to be fully in the body experiencing the pain. Many people try to get out of the body or disassociate with the body by using alcohol, drugs or food to space out or detach from their pain. Illness, disease, injury or physical abuse may cause physical pain. An example of how to detach from the pain in a healthy way is to shift your awareness to an image or thought that is comforting or pleasurable. Use deep relaxation (breathing into all the parts of your body telling the body to relax) and visualization (focusing on a pleasant image) to move your awareness from the pain.

2. Emotional pain also causes us to be ungrounded. It is common for us to disassociate from the emotional pain associated with anger, being blamed, shamed, ridiculed or invalidated. We may numb ourselves, space out, shut down or ignore something that is hurting or frightening us because we do not know how to handle the emotional pain. Most of us have learned not to feel. We hold our breath and stop the feeling. It has not been okay to feel our own anger or sadness. So, it is denied and not felt. If it is felt, we may shut the feeling down or repress it because it is not okay to express it. Emotions, especially anger, get expressed in unhealthy, hurtful ways such as through raging, shaming, blaming and violence. The message is loud and clear that it is not safe to express emotional pain, so we keep it inside. Better yet, we deny what we feel. We disconnect from our self by going numb, detaching or spacing out and not feeling anything. Then, we have no feelings to express.

3. Other people's emotions can make us ungrounded. We may not know how to handle the emotions of someone close to us so we disconnect from them and from our emotions. If someone is experiencing grief, anger, fear or sadness, we may not know how to just be with them without taking on their emotions or trying to fix it for them. Their emotional response may scare us or overwhelm us or trigger emotions we have not dealt with and do not want to face. We stop breathing and disconnect, not knowing what to do or how to help. Some people become so "other oriented" that they feel responsible and try to help, often by giving up themselves and what is good for them. When you are so concerned with the other person and "being there" for them at the expense of yourself, you lose yourself. You need to "be there" for yourself too, and take care of yourself.

We are very creative in what we do to distract ourselves from our pain, whether it is emotional or physical. Some people use drugs or alcohol, watch TV, use the Internet or play computer games, eat, shop, work and get involved with other people's lives. If you are not grounded, you will not be able to handle your emotional energy or anyone else's. If you are not in your body and present (in the now) with yourself, you cannot distinguish your feelings from the feelings of others.

Getting grounded means you need to be willing to be in present time with yourself, and be willing to feel your feelings and allow the emotional energy to flow and not be held in or pushed down. Getting grounded means that you will feel what is going on for you. Being grounded helps you let go of emotional energy, other people's stuff, and to clear and let go of your emotional "baggage." The "baggage" is the emotional pain you did not deal with (feel and express). You may have stuffed the pain from your past by denying, repressing, numbing or detaching from it.

As a child, I was very sensitive. I could feel other people's feelings. I absorbed or took on what was going on with them, and did not know what my feelings were or what I wanted because I was so concerned about making sure they were happy, especially my parents. I took on my mother's insecurity and fear of not being worthy, lovable or good enough, and I took on my father's anger.

I did not know how to deal with my parents' emotions or how to express my own feelings. I just stuffed all my feelings, and became quite confused about what I felt. Then, I shut down and did not feel, and did not know what I needed or wanted. I disconnected from myself and became "other oriented" by being a "people pleaser." My happiness was based on the people around me being happy. I only wanted what would make others happy. If asked what I wanted for dinner, my usual response was, "Whatever makes you happy or whatever you want is okay with me." I was ungrounded, scattered and confused.

How to Get Grounded

1. Take a breath and feel your body as you breathe into it. Now imagine or visualize yourself connected to the Earth like a tree that has roots running deep into the Earth from your legs and feet or imagine you have a cord that runs down from the base of your spine going deep into the Earth and anchor it in. This cord or the roots can be as big or thick, as you need them to be.

Become aware of your feet, legs, knees and pelvis. Breathe into these parts of your body.

2. Sit or lie on the Earth; walk on the Earth, the beach or take a hike; dance. Jump to bring your awareness to your legs and feet.

3. Be out in nature and hug a tree or sit on a rock. This helps to bring your attention to the Earth and your body.

4. Meditate.

Meditation

Meditation and visualization are important tools for creating and maintaining health. They are tools to help you go to the source of your problems to see clearly what is going on and get the answers you need. It is a way to become aware of yourself. Meditation helps you to become conscious of your deepest feelings and beliefs. Visualization helps you create what you want, whether it is health and well being, peace, better relationships, more money or satisfying work.

When you become quiet and relaxed, you are able to listen to yourself. You become aware of the concepts, beliefs and emotions that no longer serve you. You can then choose what to keep and what to release. Through meditation you can get in touch with what you really want.

To visualize you need only to imagine. Do not worry if you do not know how to visualize. You do not have to see a form or image in your mind's eye to imagine it. You may sense it or feel it instead. We all use our imagination differently. It is important to relax first, and then get and hold the impression, thought or image.

In meditation, begin by using your breath to relax. The breath is very important in bringing your awareness and focus to the body. When you are in pain, in fear, tense or anxious, you contract. The breath opens you up in the process of inhaling. It expands your lungs and you immediately begin to relax as you breathe deeply.

Benefits of Meditation and Relaxation

1. The body is able to rest and rejuvenate itself (blood pressure lowers, heart rate steadies, brain waves drop into an alpha state that is a slower rate and most effective in healing and creating).
2. The body comes into balance when relaxed.
3. The mind becomes calm and clear.
4. Emotions can be felt and released resulting in a feeling of calm and peace.
5. When relaxed you are able to listen to our Inner Source for guidance and wisdom.

It takes **practice** to relax, meditate and visualize. It is a *Spiritual Practice* of turning your attention inward to be aware, conscious of yourself.

Working with Earth and Universal Cosmic Energy

After creating your grounding, open to the flow of energy from the Earth and from the Universe. This Life Force energy flows through your body through a tube about the diameter of your thumb and middle finger touching each other. This *"Prana Tube"* runs through the center of your body from the base of your spine or perineum to the crown of your head bringing Life Force energy into your bubble of light (electro-magnetic energy sphere) which encompasses your entire body. Prana means life force in the Sanskrit language. The Chinese call it Chi. The Japanese call it Ki, and the Hawaiians call it Mana. The Life Force is a Divine energy you can use to heal and shift patterns in order to return to your wholeness. You can revitalize yourself with the Life Force just by bringing your awareness to the flow. You can then fill up with what you need.

Definitions:
> **Earth energy** provides stability, strength, support and nurturance. It is also very calming. If you are afraid or anxious, feeling unsupported, lonely, weak, or unable to take action, fill up with Earth energy.

Universal Cosmic energy inspires us; it uplifts, energizes, and is expansive. If you are feeling low in energy, depressed, confused, fill yourself with cosmic energy.

You generally need to have **both** Earth and Cosmic energy running or flowing through you in **balance** — 50% Earth and 50% Cosmic. You decide what you need. Hold the intention of being balanced. You may need a combination of 25% Earth and 75% Cosmic energy or vice versa depending on what you are doing. For example, when I am teaching or writing I usually have 25% Earth and 75% Cosmic energy running so that my body feels strong and I am in an expanded and inspired state of awareness. When I am doing aerobics I run about 90% Earth energy and 10% Cosmic energy.

YOUR BODY CENTERED IN THE LIGHT
OF YOUR SPIRIT with PRANA TUBE

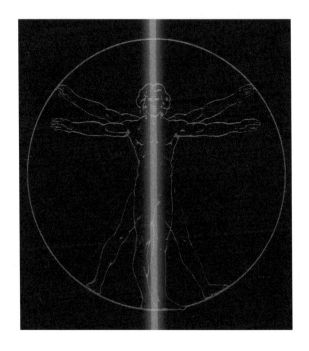

It is important to remember to stay open to the flow of the Life Force. When we are in fear we contract which stops, slows or blocks the flow of energy in and through us. Whenever you **release** fear, guilt, shame or negative thinking you need to **fill up** and **replace** what you have released with love, acceptance, courage or strength.

I recommend that whenever you ground yourself, you release what you are ready to let go and then fill up with Earth and Cosmic energy in a balance that works for you in the moment. Remember to stay open to the flow and be willing to change.

When I am being a conduit for the Life Force energy in a healing setting, I open to the flow of energy from the Earth and Universe running through my *Prana tube*. I bring the energies into balance in my heart. Next, I intend the Life Force energy to flow from my heart through my arms and hands to the person I am assisting. I hold the intention of balance or wholeness for the person and visualize a white light or color flowing into them. I do the same with myself when I am doing a healing on myself. I place my hands on the area of my body that may be in pain. Sometimes, I just focus the energy into a part of my body using visualization, intending the energy to go there.

Grounding Meditation

(Read this meditation or have a friend read it to you or record it using your own voice and play it back.)

Begin by settling into a comfortable place and take a few really deep breaths. Allow your body to begin to relax, breathing into your neck and shoulders, letting your shoulder blades slide down your back. Relaxing as you are breathing in and breathing out. Allow your awareness to move with the breath.

Imagine yourself on a place on the Earth where you feel comfortable, a place that is in harmony with you, a place that resonates with you. As you are breathing in, move your awareness down to the base of your spine, into the first chakra (energy center). Imagine the base of your spine, drop down a cord, a grounding cord or imagine the roots of a tall, strong tree going deep down into the Earth. Now, allow the cord or roots to drop deep down and anchor it in. You are now connected to the Earth, the physical plane and your physical body.

Grounding serves two purposes. 1. It connects you to the Earth, enabling you to handle your physical, emotional, mental and spiritual energy. 2. It is your release valve. You can let go of whatever it is that you need to let go of by grounding it out. The energy that you release is neutralized. It then can be transformed and recycled.

Whatever image you use to ground, know that it

connects you to your body and that you can release whatever it is that you need to let go. Grounding helps you handle your own energy. Feel yourself connected to the Earth, anchored in. feel yourself grounded. Take a few really deep breaths, in and out...feeling.

Now, begin to release. If you want to release anything, simply give it a color. If you have taken on anyone else's energy from your day, just give their energy a color, like red, and see the red draining out of you down your grounding cord. Maybe you have been feeling anxious today. Ground out the fear, the anxiety. Be willing to let it go and allow it to release through your grounding cord as you are breathing in and out, relaxing deeper and deeper into yourself with each breath you take.

After you release, it is important to fill up. Fill up with Earth energy in a proportion that feels in balance for you. The Earth energy can have any color or vibration that feels in harmony with you. You might want to fill up with the color of a meadow, the frequency of a rock or the vibration of the sand on the beach. You can even use the energy of water since that is part of the earth too.

Allow yourself to fill up with the Earth energy, drawing it up through the *Prana tube*, which runs through the center of your body from the base of your spine to the crown of your head. The *Prana tube* brings in the Life Force energy into the bubble of light (energy sphere) which encompasses your entire body. Earth energy is nurturing, calming, stable, strong and supportive. Allow the Earth energy to flow into you and fill you up your solar plexus. If there is any particular quality that you want more of, such as strength, nurturing, stability, just draw it in, and let it fill you. If there is anything else that you want to let go of, just let it flow down your grounding chord or roots. It is important to fill up after you release. There is no need to hold on or hold back. Allow the flow.

Take another really deep breath and bring your awareness to your head. See the crown of your head open like the lens of a camera or a flower opening to the sun. This time bring in Universal Cosmic energy. You can go anywhere in the universe to get it. Maybe you want energy of the sun, the moon, one of the planets or the universe itself. See that Universal Cosmic energy coming in, flowing in through the crown of your head and see it moving, feel it moving all the way through your *Prana tube* into your solar plexus.

Notice the difference between Earth energy and the Cosmic energy. If there is any particular quality that you need, fill yourself with it. Cosmic energy is uplifting, inspiring, creative and energizing. Allow yourself to open to the flow, letting go and filling up.

Now, bring up the Earth energy through your *Prana tube* all the way up to your solar plexus, and allow it to circulate. Notice how it feels. Bring in the Cosmic energy through the crown of your head, right down your *Prana tube* into your solar plexus and mix and blend it with Earth energy. Mix them in a proportion that feels in balance for you.

Combine them any way that you want. You might want an equal amount of Earth and Cosmic energy. Maybe you want more Earth energy than Cosmic energy. Choose whatever feels good to you. If there is a particular color or quality that you want in the energies, you only have to imagine it happening.

Now, circulate the energy by running it through your body. Breathe in deeply, allowing the energy to give you a healing, a cleansing throughout your body and aura (emotional body). Clearing your space. Allow the energy to run at your own pace. Grounding out what you do not need, and filling up with what you want more of in your life. Notice where the energy is moving easily, where it flows. Be aware of areas that are blocked and congested. Feel the energy flowing. Feel being grounded.

Take a deep breath in and bring your awareness back to the room, back to your body sitting. When you are ready, open your eyes being fully present, grounded with your energy flowing.

BEING CENTERED

"There is nothing to do but be."
Stephen Levine

It takes more than being grounded to live your life fully, although it is essential to be grounded. Remember you are a spirit in a body. You need to be grounded in order to be here on the Earth plane and be present to handle the affairs of your life. However, it is equally important to be centered.

"Being centered," means being in the love and compassion of your Spirit and coming from that place. You feel it in your heart. It means you are connected to your Spiritual Self which allows you to connect to all things...to feel the Oneness and interconnectedness with all living creatures and things such as animals, rocks, trees, flowers, the waters, the earth, the sun and moon, the Universe. You are the eye of the hurricane, the peaceful center. You come from your heart in your interactions with others.

Being centered is a feeling of peace, calm, fullness, warmth, stillness, quiet, relaxation, expansiveness, compassion and love. It is an interior sense of self. There is a knowing of balance and wholeness within you, a confidence in just "being" yourself. You may experience intuitive flashes or a heightened sense of awareness. There is a feeling of connection to yourself, to others and other forms of life, a sense of unity with all beings.

"Being centered" in your spiritual aspect and qualities, means moving or focusing your consciousness, your awareness on the spiritual qualities already inherent within you. You are Love, Compassion, Wisdom, Peace, Strength, Joy, Creativity, Zeal or Enthusiasm, Faith, Trust, Order, Understanding and Will. Focus on these qualities that are you. Rituals may help you to focus your awareness on your center. Use whatever centering rituals work for you. You can center yourself with just the thought, the intention, "I AM CENTERED." (More on intention in Chapter 10)

CENTERING RITUALS

Breathing consciously

Meditation

Visualization
(imagine a ball of light, any color you
choose, representing your essence,
your Spiritual Self totally enveloping you)

Prayer

Lighting a candle

Burning sage or incense

Toning

Chiming bells or gongs

**Focusing on a specific spiritual quality like
love or peace**

Being in nature

Listening to relaxing music

The Difference Between Being Grounded and Centered.

Being grounded means you are in your body. You feel present and focused like a body builder who experiences his body feeling strong and competent at the physical level. Another example is a businessman who manages money or builds things and is successful in handling earthly matters. Neither one may be connected to their heart (love and compassion) or to others. They may not have a sense of a larger connection to life. These people may be grounded, but not centered.

In contrast, you may have encountered a "spiritual" person who does not show up for appointments on time or does not manage their checkbook, who feels scattered and disorganized, and is overwhelmed by life in a body on this planet. This person may have been labeled as an "airy fairy" spiritual person. They can connect to a sense of love for others and other life forms, but cannot handle the mundane tasks of living. This person is centered but not grounded. It is essential to be both grounded and centered to be and express your authentic self.

≈SPIRITUAL PRINCIPLE≈
Ground and Center.

Being grounded and centered enables you to be present and connect to your self, your body, and your

Spiritual Self. From that connection to self/Self you are able to function in the world and experience your interconnectedness to all life. To live life from your center is like being the calm eye of a hurricane. Life's storms may come and go, yet you remain at peace within yourself and are able to handle what life presents. You can be present with those you interact with and respond with clarity. When you are centered, you are not reacting from a place of fear.

Connecting with Your Spiritual Self

The next process in being centered is connecting with your Spiritual Self, your Inner Source of Wisdom. You are more than your body, emotions, or mind. You are a Spiritual Being that has a body, mind and emotions with which to experience life.

You can consciously connect to your Spiritual aspect by intending to do so. You may call it forth. It is always with you. It is a part of you. You are within it and it is within you. You cannot be separate from it, even if you are not aware of it.

Imagine your Spiritual Self as a symbol, a form (either a person, animal or geometric form), a color, a feeling or sense, or an energy that moves within you or around you. Allow it to come into your awareness. Feel, see, or sense its presence with you. Open yourself to experience it communicating with you.

~SPIRITUAL PRINCIPLE~
All the Answers are within You.

Be open. Listen. Trust. Take action on the guidance given to you. In order to know the answer, you need only to ask and listen. You honor your Spirit by listening, trusting and acting upon the guidance you receive.

~SPIRITUAL PRINCIPLE~
Honor Your Spirit.

When you honor your Spirit you are respecting and valuing yourself. You are recognizing what you need and feel is important. Honoring yourself allows you to live a life that is real and authentic. It means doing and expressing what comes from your heart, your deepest truth.

Centering Meditation
(Read this meditation, have a friend read it to you or
record it using your own voice and play it back)

Take a few deep breaths, allow yourself to settle in and
begin to relax. Focus on breathing in and breathing out.
Put down your grounding and feel yourself connecting
deep into the Earth, anchoring yourself into a place in the
Earth where you feel safe, where you feel in harmony.
Begin to let go, grounding out (releasing) anything that
you are ready to let go. Clearing out your space by letting
go of anyone else's energy that you might have taken on.
Letting go of anything you may be holding against
yourself or anyone else like judgment, guilt, hurt, fear.
Releasing and opening to the flow of energy from the
Earth and Universe through your *Prana tube* to fill you.
Bring the energy of the Earth and Universe together in
your solar plexus in a balance that is appropriate for you.
Feeling the flow of Universal Life Force energy filling you
with what you need. Just allowing it in.

Allow energy to flow, run, and circulate through your
body. Now, move your awareness to your heart space, and
imagine a small pinpoint of light right there in the center
of your heart and see this light beginning to expand out,
filling your heart. See the light fill all of your body and
then imagine that your body is in the light, centered and
enveloped and surrounded in the light. Your awareness is
in the center of your being, your light, the center of your
own love. You are centered in your joy. Centered in your

peace. Centered in your strength. Centered in your wisdom. Centered in your Divine Self. Grounded and centered. Breathe deep into your center. Being filled up with the light.

When you are centered you are connected with yourself and all of life. Open your awareness to feel your connection to all things and beings. Feel the love that is you radiating out from your heart and flowing within you.

From this centered place, connect with your Spiritual Self, the Divine aspect of you that is your wisdom, your knowing, and your intuition. It is the part of you that guides you. You can call forth this part by imagining it or giving it a form. You can create a symbol that represents your Spirit or Divine Self. It might come to you as a ball of light, or in the form of a person, an animal, a geometric shape, or it might be a feeling. Whatever or however it comes does not matter. Know that it represents your Higher Self, that Divine part of you that knows. The form might even change, but get to know how it communicates with you. Call it forth now, and let it come in whatever form it takes, and if no form comes, just make one up, imagine it.

Ask whatever form comes, "Do you represent my Spiritual Self?" Listen for the answer. If another form comes and says for example, "No, I am not, I am your mother's voice," then, just let it go and ask once again for your Spiritual Self to appear to you. **Ask it to communicate to you in ways you can understand**.

Your Spiritual Self can give you answers. You need only ask. So, if you are confused about something, ask for clarity. If you have to make a decision, not knowing which direction to take, which way to turn, **ask**. If there is an issue that you want more information about, ask. If you want to know what the fear is really about, ask. If you want to know an area where you feel stuck, ask. If you want to know about your value or worth, your lovability, **ask your Spiritual Self**. Your Spiritual Self is here to guide you. Let your Spiritual Self know that you are willing to communicate, that you want to listen, and that you are willing to act on the guidance. When you listen and you act, trust develops within yourself. Now, ask whatever it is you want to know. Ask your Spiritual Self if there is anything that it wants to tell you that you need to know at this time.

Listen. If you need more clarification, ask. If your Spiritual Self gives you a symbol or an image or a message that you do not quite understand, then ask for more understanding. Open yourself to listen. Be willing to know. The answers are here within you.

Acknowledge yourself for taking the time to listen within. In gratitude, thank your Spiritual Self for coming to speak with you. Your Spiritual Self speaks in many ways. The more you listen, the more you will know.

Bring your awareness back to your body by taking a few deep breaths. Breathe deeply into your body, and become aware of the room. Check your grounding to make sure you are anchored in. Let go any fear that may have come up from any of the messages or information that has come forth. Know that it is okay to be afraid. Sometimes, we are guided to grow or expand in ways that we have not been moving in, and we get scared. Just know that you can release the fear. Breathe in deeply, making sure you are grounded and your energy is flowing. Now, begin to move your toes and fingers, do a little stretch throughout your body. Open your eyes when your ready, being fully grounded and centered.

Profound Change

Connection with your Spiritual Self is profound, and changes will occur in your life. The following is a story of a couple married 16 years and on the verge of divorce. They came to a retreat in Hawaii that I was co-facilitating with Alan Cohen, and they were already behaving separately. They did not share accommodations, sit or talk with each other. No one realized they were a couple. During the course of the retreat they both had individual counseling and energy work healings with me. It was during our interaction that the wife connected to her Spiritual Self. The husband also connected with himself by getting grounded and bringing his Soul essence into his body. This was the beginning of great changes for each of them in their personal selves and in their marriage. One year later I received a letter from the wife describing some of the their changes.

Dear Sharon,

The impact of the words you spoke to me are with me still. I am different, so different a year later all because you helped me connect to my Spiritual Self. You saw beyond how scattered I appeared at the time. You saw my authentic self, even though I could not see me. You told me my marriage could work and that it would be good with renewed passion and love. At the time, everything seemed in shambles and so hopeless. I thought I wanted to end my marriage and be free. Hearing from my Spirit that I needed to stay in the marriage and that it could work sounded so unbelievable, but I trusted.

I came back home from the retreat and ended my affair within three days. I locked myself in my house and had an emotional breakdown. I felt desperate and hollow, and experienced great sadness. The pain was overwhelming at times. I did not leave my house for six weeks.

In the midst of all this, every day my husband and I had these awesome conversations. I told him all of my painful secrets and hateful feelings and we discovered the great joy on the other side of telling the truth and shedding layers.

Two months passed, and I woke up one day and realized I was in love with my husband. I do not speak that word lightly. I felt all the feelings of being in love. I put my ring back on that day. Now, we are both being our true selves, and showing ourselves to each other. Some days are emotionally overwhelming, but the good is constant. We meditate and have learned to do Reiki (energy work) healings that we give to each other and our children.

Thank you Sharon for opening the gateway to Spirit and giving me hope. What greater gift?

Love, L

DISCOVERING LIFE'S PURPOSE

*"Everyone has a purpose in life...a unique gift
or special talent to give to others."*
Deepak Chopra

Many people ask the question, "Why am I here in this body on the earth and living this life? Why am I going through all this?" There must be a reason or purpose for living. There is. Life's events such as death, divorce, job changes and illness are fertile ground that present opportunities for growth and change. These events may lead us to the answers as they bring a greater awareness of our true or authentic self. The lessons of life contain wisdom our souls need to learn.

All it takes to discover your life's purpose is to ask the question, "What is my Soul's purpose in this life? What am I here to learn or do?" After asking the question, be open to receive the answer.

Discovering My Life's Purpose

The path of my journey to self-discovery and knowing who I truly am led me to question my life's purpose and ask why I am here?" I wanted to know in order to live life to the fullest.

You do not have to experience a crisis in your life in order to get the message, but sometimes it takes a crisis to get your attention, as it did for me. My near-death experience woke me up and enabled me to listen to the answers that were within me. Up to that point, I had been asking, but not listening.

Before my near-death experience, I wanted to know what my real work was instead of the various jobs I was doing. What would I do when I grew up? My background and education led me into a traditional counseling setting working with teenagers and their families. I stopped because I was burned out emotionally. I didn't know how to set *boundaries* (saying "yes" to what I wanted and "no" to what I don't want). I took a job working in the insurance industry as a manager, and wondered if there was anything in life that could fulfill me.

After my near-death experience, I went into a state of depression for six months. I kept wondering, "Why I was alive and why I didn't die? What am I supposed to do now? What is my life's purpose?"

I was feeling suicidal. However, I did not plan on taking my own life. Instead, while walking in the woods I would ask God to take me back to the light. In nature, I felt closer to God and somewhat at peace, yet I wanted out of this life. I wanted to go back to the love and peace I experienced upon dying.

My life was not what I wanted it to be. I was in an unhappy marriage with an alcoholic husband I did not trust. I felt depressed because I had no chance of having a baby.

My husband accepted a job on the East Coast the week I came home from the hospital. He left me with the decision to join him or not. If I chose to go, I would have to leave my hometown, my house, my job, family and friends. I hadn't told him the truth about the pregnancy. It was too much loss all at once. I was faced with this situation the week after coming home from the hospital! I was in such grief. How could I leave everything and go be with this man I loved but did not trust? There were so many lies between us.

Unhappily, I moved three months later to join my husband. I was so despondent I stayed away from people, especially children. My life was in shambles. This was my third marriage, and it was not working. Yet, I was willing to give it another try. Through all this, I kept asking, "Why am I alive?"

After the near-death experience, I began to look at my relationship, my life and myself. I looked at it all. For six months, I asked the question, "Why am I alive?" The answer came in a way I never expected. It did not come the many times I would go into the woods, crawl underneath bushes and lie on the ground praying to die. I would feel myself melting into the earth and wished it would swallow me up. I felt the strength of the earth beneath me as I lay under the protective cover that hid me from the world. I could not hide from God or myself any longer. Hours would pass and I would feel comforted, more peaceful and relaxed.

The answer did not come right away when I called out to God. I do not know how I expected it to come, certainly not from within since I had spent my life looking to others for answers. For most of my life I had thought God was outside of me.

The discovery of my life's purpose came when I went for a healing because I was depressed and suicidal. I needed help. Fortunately, I met a woman in Philadelphia who was learning Therapeutic Touch healing (laying on of hands and working with the electro-magnetic energy field of the body). She offered me a healing session. Since I had gone to psychics and spiritual healers several times in the past I accepted.

There were two women practicing Therapeutic Touch together on me. During the healing, it was as if a light bulb went on as the insight came. It was an "aha" experience, an inner message in the form of words spoken directly to me from God.

I felt a rush of warmth and love flood my body. I started to cry. A still small voice inside me and around me spoke and said, "This is the work you are to do.   Be the healer that you are. It is time to heal your heart and leave this loveless marriage. Learn to love yourself and be the love that you are, and extend that love to others."   I had received a "calling" from God. I realized in that moment that healing work was to be a form of my expression and purpose.

I felt joy as I recognized Spirit speaking to me, and embraced my purpose.   It was the answers to my questions. Now, I knew what to do but not how do it? Feeling happiness, sorrow, relief and fear at the same time. I asked, "How am I going to accomplish this, heal my heart and leave my marriage?"

That week, six months after nearly dying, I accepted my life and chose to move forward and change. I enrolled in a Therapeutic Touch healing class and went into therapy. I knew I needed help to change my co-dependent behavior of taking care of others at the expense of myself, and looking for validation from others. I needed to heal my wounded heart, increase my self-esteem, and learn to tell the truth. I had to learn how to listen and trust myself.

I knew I needed help to change and I went into therapy and received energy work healings.   There was much I needed to learn such as loving and accepting myself, forgiving myself and others, how to stop living for others and meeting their needs before my own, and how to take care of myself. I was ready to once again begin the process of self-acceptance and self-expression. I chose the process of getting healthy. I chose and still choose to live and fully be myself, to be authentic!

Connecting with Your Soul

Sit in meditation. Ground yourself. Breathe into your heart—centering yourself in love. Then, move your awareness to the crown of your head and call forth your Soul. Let your Soul come in whatever form or symbol it comes. Ask what you need to know. Allow yourself to receive impressions. You may get an intuitive knowing or vision or direct message from your Soul during the meditation. If you need help, call upon your Spiritual Self, your Divine Aspect, your Inner Source of Wisdom that knows all. Through practice in contacting your Soul, you will become familiar with your own essence, which has its own vibration, frequency or color. Be open to communication from your Soul. If you do not receive information during the meditation, that is okay. The answer may come when you are hiking in the woods, driving your car or doing the dishes.

Soul's Purpose

Many times we think our soul's purpose is some grand thing we must do like save the world, stop pollution or world hunger, or assist in uplifting human consciousness. However, the purpose for our soul may be to learn the lesson of loving yourself, being patient, raising a family with joy, giving our voice to a cause that touches our heart, or developing some new device that makes living easier. The soul may want to experience surfing, hiking, painting, gardening, sky diving, or even disease. What the soul wants to experience may not be one thing, but many. The soul is creatively evolving from and through many experiences. Remember: *All the answers are within you.* You need only to ask what your purpose is, then listen.

Exercise: Soul's Purpose Meditation and Journal

Sit in meditation. Ground and Center yourself. Call forth your Soul and Spiritual Self and **ask within to know your Soul's purpose**. Then, **listen for the answer**. The answer is the vision or goal (purpose) of what you are here to do and learn. The following are questions to ask. Write in a journal the information you receive after you come out of meditation.

1. What is the **personal vision** for my soul? This has to do with your personal life lessons and growth in the evolvement of your soul.

Example: You are learning how to be loving and accepting of self and others by releasing judgment.

2. What is the **world vision** for my soul? This has to do with how you contribute to the larger whole.

Example: Assisting others in learning to value life.

3. What is your **professional vision?** Is your work in alignment with your personal and world vision?

Example: Teaching others to be tolerant of cultural differences at a university.

4. What are your **guiding principles and values?** These will keep you on the path and going in the direction in alignment with your purpose.

Example: Principle — All the answers are within.
Values — Being accepting of yourself and others, respecting yourself and others, being considerate and kind.

5. What are your **goals?** (one week to 3-5 years) These are the intentions you set to achieve and live your vision (purpose). Are these in alignment with your personal and world vision?

Examples: Being considerate of those I encounter each day. Develop a meditation practice. Respect others and myself This year take a course in cross-cultural counseling. Two years from now apply for a job at a university.

6. What **action steps** are you willing to commit to do that will lead to the creation of your short-term goals?

Examples: Meditate daily on loving others and myself, accept others and myself by stopping the put downs, get information on classes and job possibilities, and fill out an application for job.

WHAT TO DO WHEN
GOD CALLS

*"All I have seen teaches me to trust the Creator
for all I have not seen."*
Ralph Waldo Emerson

Are you listening to Spirit? What do you do when God calls? Do you recognize you are receiving a message from God or Spirit? How does the message come to you? How do you respond? Do you trust the message or guidance? What obstacles or resistance arise?

Working as a healing practitioner, spiritual life counselor and teacher in Santa Barbara, California, I was being interviewed on a local television show called "What do you do when God calls?" The questions above were asked of me. I said, "First, you have to recognize that you are receiving a message." The host asked me, "How do you get messages, guidance or intuitions?" I answered, "It is different for all of us. It is individual, yet there are some common ways we all may experience intuitive guidance." I then went on to explain:

"Some of us have a gut feeling about something. It just feels right or wrong or off in our gut, stomach or solar plexus region. You may have a feeling in your heart. You may just know. You may not know how you know. It may not make any sense, but you know. Others may just have a sense that something is for them. It can be a physical sensation in the body like goose bumps, a chill or a rush of electricity running through the body. You may also hear a message. It can come as a voice or maybe a sound or tone that lets you know that something is for you. Some people see the message in the form of a vision. Then, they may have to rely on other senses to interpret what the vision means for them. You may experience all these ways or just one."

The word "vocation" comes from the Latin *vocare*, which means "to call". There is a difference between a job, a career and a "calling." A calling comes from within you, your soul essence. You must respond or life seems meaningless. Sarah Ban Breathnach, author of *Simple Abundance* puts it this way: "Realize Spirit has no hands, head, or heart like yours. No other on earth can do what you alone are called to do, can give to the world what you alone were sent to give through your authentic gifts."

All of us receive messages from within. You do not have to be psychic to get messages, even though we all have some abilities. A person who is psychic gets information for others. They are clairvoyant or can "see." An intuitive person receives message for himself or herself. We are all intuitive.

How To Access Your Intuition

Spirit speaks to us in many ways. Spirit may communicate as a still small voice or as a knowing or a feeling within you. A message may come when a person says just what you need to hear. It may come while you are browsing in a bookstore and a book falls off the shelf. You pick it up, and it is exactly what you need. You may get a feeling or sensation in your gut. A message may come when you are at a movie and something is said that touches your heart, inspires you, or imparts a precious gem of wisdom. An insight or vision may come to you when you are washing dishes or driving your car. This happens to me a lot. I also get messages when walking in nature or sitting in meditation.

You can experience messages as a feeling, a sense or sensation in your body, a vision, or by hearing a sound or voice. There can be more than one way that you receive guidance. Are you listening? Do you recognize that your Intuition (Spirit) is communicating with you in these forms?

The most common question is: "Whose voice is this I

am hearing?" This is a good question to ask, as you need to discern the voices that are inside your head. Is it the voice of your mother or father, a teacher, cultural or religious programming? Is it the voice of Spirit?

The voice of Spirit does not have a "should" or "have to" on it. It does not judge you, make you feel small or less than. There is a sense of power or peace to the message inside of you. It may come as a quiet or loud voice, but there is stillness, a peace or calmness to it. It has a feeling of love or rightness, an excitement, or an energy running through the body that stimulates.

When I first recognized that Spirit was giving me messages it usually was a feeling or I heard a message. Through practice, I developed my other intuitive senses more fully, and am now able to access information by knowing, seeing, hearing, feeling and sensing.

As a child, I was aware of what others were feeling. In fact, I usually did not know the difference between someone else's feelings and my own. I just took on other's emotions and thought they were mine. It got to be confusing at times because I did not understand why my mood would change so dramatically. It was as if I were a sponge that soaked up whatever was going on in someone else. They would feel better, and I would feel worse, drained and out of sorts.

I was a sensitive. My family called me overly sensitive, and I felt bad about myself. It was not okay to know what others were feeling and experiencing, yet I somehow knew things, felt them, and even saw things. Wanting the approval of my father and to be a good little girl, I shut down my abilities. I continued to be an emotional sponge, and did not trust what I received until around age 35, when I learned to ground, release, and center myself.

It is common for children to be open to their intuitive abilities, until they are invalidated for what they know and experience. Their experiences are put into the realm of imagination, and pooh-poohed. The message received by most children is that it is definitely not okay to be intuitive.

When I started hearing messages while receiving a healing from a Therapeutic Touch healing practitioner, it was as if someone was talking to me inside my head. I remembered hearing this "voice" at other times in my life. I usually did not pay attention or pretended I did not hear anything as I shook my head or rubbed my ear. I remembered hearing this voice just before I got married to my third husband in 1979. The voice told me not to marry this man. I also had a feeling of foreboding in the pit of my stomach. I just shrugged off the voice as wedding jitters. I did not listen or trust what I was experiencing and went ahead with the wedding. Big mistake!

What Happens When You Get A Message?

Most of the time when we get a message we become fearful, usually before we experience the power of the message. We tend to mistrust, discount or invalidate the message especially if our intuitive abilities were invalidated as children. If somehow the message is received, the most common response is fear. We are fearful of change and of the unknown.

What do you do if you are afraid? Most of us hold our breath. So, the **first** thing to do when you notice you are afraid is to **breathe**. Be aware by noticing where you might be experiencing a contraction in your body. Do you feel tight in your stomach, your chest or your throat. Breathe. Breathing opens you so the energy can flow. The very process of breathing relaxes and calms you. Your body opens to receive the air. This increases the blood flow and the energy of the emotion of fear begins to move. All emotion (energy in motion) wants to move, to flow like a river down to the sea.

We go out of balance when we hold back, repress or shut down and deny the emotion that we are experiencing. Accept what it is you are feeling. Breathe into it. Breathe into the part of your body that is contacted. Tell yourself it is okay to be afraid of change or the unknown. It is okay to be afraid. You are human.

Next, tell yourself you will be okay. Keep breathing as you tell yourself you can do it, handle it, or make it through. When Spirit is guiding you do to something it will show you as to how you can do it. Step by step, you will be guided. Breathe and tell yourself you are okay and that you will be okay. This creates safety and peace for you in your body and mind. Breathing calms the emotions and moves the emotional energy so it does not get stuck in the body.

You will be guided step by step. Spirit will bring the right person or people into your life to assist you, teach you or work with you. You may be guided to the perfect book, seminar or class that further develops new skills for what you are called to do. It all happens synchronistically. Pay attention to the little signals and signs that are there to help you.

Be patient with yourself as you are uncovering and moving through your fear and limiting thoughts. Release the thoughts that tell you, "You cannot do it or be it." Recognize you are in a process of change. Are you willing to change? Most humans like things to stay as they are, even if they are uncomfortable. Change is scary. The familiar is comfortable even if we are suffering.

As for me, my change was to leave my marriage and begin a healing program in Therapeutic Touch. Trusting the guidance, I enrolled in a healing program that week. I began to remember. I opened to my intuitive abilities and began to listen and trust myself.

> ~SPIRITUAL PRINCIPLE~
> *Listen, Trust, Take Action.*

The biggest challenge for most of us is to learn to trust. It certainly was for me. I was used to not listening and not trusting. I would look to others to have the answers for me or to tell me what to do. Trusting myself and Spirit helped me change my life.

Most of us get messages from Spirit, but we do not trust the message or the information, and then we do not act on it. Developing trust is a process. It begins by taking small steps that lead us to larger steps. Trusting can sometimes feel like you are jumping off a cliff when guided to do something seemingly outrageous. When there is trust, you can let go and jump, trusting that all will work out. Know that you will not only survive but that you will thrive.

Trust is built. When you listen, trust and take action, you will experience peace instead of anxiety or fear. When you trust, you will feel love and fulfillment. When you do not listen or trust your life can be filled with lots of drama, fear, pain, and heartache. Once you begin the habit of listening, trusting and taking action, your life will get easier. The more you trust the easier it is to trust. Learn to trust in small ways first. Then, when the big things come along such as being guided to change your life by moving to another city, ending a relationship or changing careers, it will be easier because the foundation of trust is there.

Listen to your body. What food, rest, and activity level does it want? Give it what it wants and needs. **Listen to your intuition** about who to be with, what to wear, where to go, which book to read or movie to watch, which job to take, or what form your creativity wants to express. **Trust and take action.**

Know it will be all right. Your life will work out. You will be okay. I recommend listening and trusting Spirit, and taking the appropriate action. What a way to live your life!

∾SPIRITUAL PRINCIPLE∾
You are 100% Responsible for Your Life.

Being 100% responsible for your life means to stop blaming others and accept and own your part in a situation or interaction. Realize you can choose to change your thinking and perceptions about yourself and your life situation, and your feelings will change too. You can start to see that your life reflects what you believe. You are 100% responsible for your thoughts, reaction and actions. Are you reacting from fear or acting from love? Are your reactions based on thoughts (beliefs) that limit you or empower you? It is your choice. Change your thinking.

Taking 100% responsibility for my life lead me to therapy. I needed to heal my heart and learn how not to give my power away to others to please them to get their approval or love. I learned how to trust myself, own my own feelings, let go responsibility for other's happiness or their feelings, say no to what I do not want and yes to what I do want.

It took me two years to get healthy enough to leave the marriage I was guided by Spirit to leave. I had many beliefs to change, behaviors to unlearn, and a lot of fear to face. I had to learn many new ways of being. It took time before I was empowered enough to be on my own. However, I took steps in that direction by remembering and trusting the message often. Thank God I wrote the message down so I could not pretend I did not get it! I knew somewhere deep inside me it was what was best for me even though I was scared.

THE CALLING

When I was first called to do healing work, something inside me said Yes. This was the answer to my questions "Why am I here? and what is my purpose?" When the answer came I was afraid that I did not know how to do healing work. I was not healthy enough or healed enough myself. I was not worthy of being a healing practitioner. Why would anyone come to me? All these doubts came up before I went to my first healing class. Fortunately, Spirit had already provided help for me immediately after I received the calling that night. One of the Therapeutic Touch healing practitioners told me a class was beginning that very week. So, I enrolled. I was afraid, but I did it anyway.

During the class, I had the feeling that I knew how to work with healing energy. It felt familiar to me. I was remembering. However, I needed to learn many new techniques and new ways of being. I knew my life was changing. I wanted it to change, even though I did not know how it would look. I knew I wanted to be out of emotional pain and be fulfilled. I wanted peace. I wanted my alcoholic, philandering husband to love me and be faithful. I wanted to do God's work. So, here I am hearing that I am to leave my marriage, heal my heart and do healing work. I began with the healing class first. Taking one step at a time.

I was shown the other steps to take from finding the right therapist to a body worker to help me clear emotions from my body. Book after book appeared in my life for me to read, and spiritual development classes kept me on the path. I felt like I was in spiritual graduate school as my body, emotions, mind and spirit were being cleared and expanded. I was learning to trust and experiencing more joy and peace than ever before. I also was experiencing more sadness and anger as the emotions cleared. This time I allowed myself to be with what I was experiencing instead of denying, repressing or shutting down the feelings. I had learned how to be present, grounded and centered within myself, and not give myself away by always focusing on others.

After two years, my trust had deepened significantly and I was healthier, speaking my truth, setting boundaries, feeling I was valuable and no longer accepting emotional and verbal abuse.

Then, the big opportunity came to me. I was walking home from the train after work in Philadelphia. Spirit spoke to me in a loud voice, "It is now time to start your healing practice. Quit your job and return to Minnesota".

I said to God, "You must be kidding. You know I do not like cold weather and Minnesota is really, really cold especially in the winter. God, you know it is December. It is cold enough for me here in Philadelphia. If I have to start over, can it be some place warm? I am not going to Minnesota!"

Since the calling to be a healing practitioner, I had been learning and practicing the healing arts and working on myself. Also, I had been praying to know the right time to start my healing practice and quit my management position. I had anticipated I would continue working in Philadelphia where I already had developed a clientele. However, this was not God's plan for me.

I was in resistance for three days. The message kept coming. On the third day with my head splitting from a migraine headache, I surrendered. I said, "Okay God, I will move back to Minnesota. Just show me how this is all going to work."

The voice of Spirit came to me telling me a psychic healer in Minneapolis would help me get started. I was given the date to quit my job and told that it all would work out.

So, I called the psychic healer whom I had not seen for ten years. I told her about my message and asked her to check with her Inner Guidance to see if it was right for her to help me. She said, "Yes!" She needed help desperately because she had a three-month waiting list of clients wanting readings and energy work healings. She said she had been praying for help, and she would refer clients to me!

Next, I called my older brotherLeRoy, in Minneapolis, who had always been a support for me and shared my interest in metaphysics. I told him I was being guided to move back home to Minnesota. He was elated! He offered to come and help move me back. Then, he offered his home to me. My cat and I lived with his family until I got my practice going and was able to support myself financially. Both he and his wife Claudia were so generous and believed in what I was doing and me. Their faith in God and me helped me tremendously. I knew it was all unfolding in Divine Order. I had no idea this was the way it would all work out.

So, what do you do when God calls? **Listen.** **Trust** that it will all work out even if you can not see how or imagine what the steps are. It will all unfold as you take each step. **Say," Yes! " Take Action.**

Trusting and Following the Guidance

Several times in my life I have been guided to take a quantum leap. I was living in St. Paul, Minnesota with family and friends around me and a healing practice that supported me. I felt a need to move and was asking Spirit to guide me to the appropriate place to live. I was imagining a place near water, maybe one of the many lakes in the area. The answer I received was not what I expected.

"Go to Sedona", was the guidance from Spirit. Now, I do not really like the desert. Warm weather? Yes! I called a friend of mine who lived in Payson, Arizona not far from Sedona. We had gone through Therapeutic Touch training together on the East Coast and had not seen each other in several years. She was thrilled that I had called and invited me to come visit her. She would show me Sedona. So, off I went not wanting to move to Arizona, but willing to check it out and see if it felt right once I got there.

We toured around Sedona and the power spots of Bell Rock, Cathedral Rock and Oak Creek Canyon, feeling the intensity and power of this sacred land. However, I was not getting any feelings of confirmation or messages to let me know this was the place to move.

That night as we went to bed I said, "I am going to sleep on this, and maybe in the morning, I will be clear and have the answer." When I woke up, I asked my friend to check in with her guidance on where I needed to move. We both went into meditation to ask. Simultaneously we came out of meditation and said, "Maui." Unbelieving I said, "I am to move to Maui, Hawaii! I had never thought about Hawaii. It was not even in my consciousness. Why Maui?" Something in my heart got excited and I said, "Yes!" I remembered I had wanted to live in the tropics when I was a seven-year-old child. I had thought God had made a mistake birthing me to my parents in Minnesota. I never liked cold weather. Could this be the fulfillment of a long held heart's desire?

Coming to the desert proved to be the place I needed to be in order to get further information. I needed to be in the desert to get clear. I was guided to go to the desert on several other significant occasions when I needed to get clear messages. The desert opens me in a subtle way enabling me to receive clear messages.

I left Arizona with clarity and an intention to follow the guidance and move to Maui. I needed to research Maui. I had no idea what it was like. Was there an airport, a city, a need for healing practitioners, or was it just jungle and beaches? A client of mine came in one day soon after

I returned from Sedona. He told me his two sisters were living on Maui. I had not even mentioned my intention to move there. It just came up as he was talking about his family. I got their names and called them to get answers to my many questions. They invited me to come visit. So, I did.

The confirmation came the first morning I was on Maui. I got up and went out on the deck to meditate. The view was breathtaking from upcountry in Kula as I overlooked the valley below and the mist covered West Maui mountains in the distance. The mountain air was cold, and not what I had expected. This was not warm and tropical. I felt a warmth and exhilaration as I cuddled into the blanket that covered me. I opened to Spirit to ask if this is what my heart desires and the place I am to live. The answer came quick, "Yes." I felt a chill run through me, though not from the cold.

Later, I took a hike up the mountain in the crisp morning air with the sunlight streaming between the tall eucalyptus trees. My sense of coming home was very strong. In this place, I can have all of what I want, the mountains, the woods, the jungle, the rolling hills, the ocean, the exotic flowers and the support of a loving group of people. The energy was so intense I leaned up against a tree, but fell to my knees in tears. Crying and laughing I consciously had to open myself to take it all in, saying, "There is so much for me here. I can have it. I am receiving it."

Yes, there was fear when I went back to Minnesota to finish teaching my classes, save money to move, and slowly disengage from my clients. I knew that Spirit was guiding me to each unfolding step. I was given four months to move. It was to be on my fortieth birthday. Time to begin my life anew. Trust.

As I continued to trust, many synchronistic events continued to happen. While still in Minnesota, I met Alan Cohen, a well-known author and lecturer in the spiritual development field. Meeting Alan was like meeting a brother from a past life. We knew we were to help and support each other. He opened his heart to me and offered me a landing place on Maui by letting me stay in his home for my first month there. He was going to be off-island on a book tour, so I would have quiet seclusion as I settled into island life.

Alan became a friend and mentor. I began doing healing sessions that included energy work, and counseling at his retreats on the Big Island. Later, I co-facilitated with him in leading retreats in Hawaii. My healing practice was slow to build on Maui, and I traveled to the mainland teaching Therapeutic Touch healing and spiritual principles.

I came to realize that I was guided to Hawaii for my own personal healing too. There were patterns from my family and more childhood hurts that needed to be released. My body was in need of clearing and balancing. I began a cleansing program to clear Candida (overgrowth of yeast) from my body. I used my two years living on Maui to focus on myself and not just on others.

I had to trust each step of the way. The more I trusted, the easier it was to trust again. Remember trust is built.

FEAR, FEAR GO AWAY

"Your task is not to seek for love, but to find
the barriers in yourself that you
have built against it."
The Course In Miracles

There are some emotions that many people do not want to feel. They will do most anything not to feel fear, anger, sadness, guilt and shame. These emotions are seen as negative and they get repressed, denied, held in and shut down. What do you do to handle the emotions you experience? Emotions are energy in motion. Emotions need to be felt and allowed to move through us. Emotions that get stuck, held in or down, denied, and repressed create an imbalance and make us depressed and sick. To move the energy, all we have to do is breathe.

Exercise: **Allow Your Emotions to Move**

1. **Breathe.** Take a long full breath that fills your abdomen, then upper chest. Slowly exhale completely emptying your lungs.
2. **Feel.**
3. **Tell yourself it is okay to feel what you feel.** Do not try to stop the feelings or shut them feelings down. Allow the feeling to move through you with the breath.
4. **Identify the thought or belief** you are thinking that contributes to the emotion.

FEAR

What happens when you are afraid? When you are scared, you contract. The simple process of breathing opens you up. When you open to the energy of the fear the emotion begins to move through you.

Next, tell yourself you are going to be **okay**. Fear is the result of thinking that something from the past or in the future is happening or is going to happen. Ask yourself, "Is it happening now?"

∼SPIRITUAL PRINCIPLE∼
The Present Moment Is All There Is.

Stay in present time and stop thinking scary thoughts. Stop thinking thoughts that make you less than, not good enough, not lovable or not capable. Your thoughts affect your emotions. You can control your thoughts. Shift your perception. Affirm that you are safe and that you are okay. Look at what you believe is going to happen. Ask yourself, "Is this the truth or just old programming from the culture, my family or my past experience?" Allow your future to be different from the past.

When you perceive yourself as being threatened it is usually because you are not accepting yourself. You fear that the other person is not accepting, liking or approving of you and withdrawing their love, abandoning you or in some way hurting you. This scares you. You stop breathing and muscles contract in your body. You feel anxious and afraid. When you do not listen to your needs and criticize yourself, you abandon and hurt yourself. What is the pain you feel? Is it the hurt of feeling unlovable and not good enough; the fear of feeling powerless and out of control; the hurt of being disappointed; or the pain of feeling unworthy—not knowing your value?

Addictions

Addictions, whether to food (carbohydrates and sugars), drugs, alcohol, cigarettes, shopping, sex, work, television or computers are an attempt not to feel the pain. Addictions distract us from the pain and temporarily make us feel good. In the end, addictions make us feel worthless, powerless and awful. We must challenge the pain, not the substance by feeling the depth of the pain.

In order to heal we must *feel.* Be willing to feel. When we feel the pain and breathe through the pain the emotion moves through us and is released. Next, change your thoughts and make choices to create a fuller life to be who you want to be. To be our true authentic self we must love ourselves enough to use our will in the moment to feel. If you are experiencing fear, feel it. Next...

〜SPIRITUAL PRINCIPLE〜
Shift Your Perception from Fear to Love.

Change the thought. Stop perceiving yourself as being in a threatening or dangerous situation. You can choose to continue creating your life as it is. But, if you do not like it, you can change it by changing your perceptions, your beliefs, and your thoughts. Look at where you learned what you think. Let go of that thought if it no longer works for you. Affirm that you are lovable and valuable. Affirm that you do have enough love, money, time or whatever you need. "I will make it and I will be okay."

When you are conscious (aware) of your beliefs you are at *choice*. Realizing you have a choice gives you power. You move out of victim consciousness (the world and life is against you) into self-empowerment (I can do it). You can choose to look at a situation, another person or yourself differently. You can then choose what brings you more joy, peace or love.

∽SPIRITUAL PRINCIPLE∽
Choice Empowers You.

Sometimes we are afraid to choose. We are afraid that our choice will hurt or disappoint someone else. We are afraid of disapproval and abandonment.

Setting *boundaries* is making a choice. A boundary is simply saying "yes" to what you want and "no" to what you do not want. Setting boundaries is taking care of yourself. A boundary says you care enough about yourself to make yourself happy by doing what you want to do.

Many people believe it is selfish to take care of oneself. Jesus said, "Love your neighbor as yourself." That means you must love yourself first so that you can love others. It means love yourself enough that you do not give up yourself or sacrifice yourself just to please someone else so they will love you and not leave you. It means loving yourself enough to honor, value and respect yourself and then treat others with the same honor, value and respect.

Setting a boundary means you have the courage to say no to what hurts you; no to abuses; no to those who take advantage of you; no to what you do not want to do. **Love yourself enough to say no.**

Tell yourself that it will be okay if others do not approve of your choice. It is okay if they do not like, understand or agree with your choice. It is okay if they are disappointed. Maybe, you are choosing something they do not agree with which scares them. Let them handle their own feelings. Each of us is responsible for our own feelings and our own perceptions. It is important to be true to yourself.

Say, "Yes, I want to do this because it gives me joy, fulfillment, pleasure, and it is what I want." Now, you are in your power. Choice gives you power. When you are in your power, there is no room for fear.

ANGER

What do you do when you are angry? Do you scream, yell in a rage, blame, become violent, hold anger in, get quite, brood, or isolate yourself? When you are angry, you may really be feeling hurt or scared. Underneath anger is hurt. Sometimes it is difficult to allow the feelings of hurt or fear and the feeling of anger is the result. But, anger is a cue that something else is going on. Anger is a wonderful energy that arises to let us know we want something different. It is the energy that mobilizes us to say, "Stop. This is hurting me or scaring me."

Many of us are afraid of how anger gets expressed. Anger expressed through rage, blaming and violence terrifies us. We are unsure how to handle it if someone is bombarding us with their rage. Even more terrifying is the volatile rage within us that we fear and must hold in. When anger is internalized, it can cause an imbalance turning into depression or illness.

When someone is dumping their anger or targeting you, learn to hold your ground and allow the other person's anger to flow past you. Do not take it in. If you do take it in, then release it by grounding yourself and letting it flow through you into the Earth. Listen to their expression of anger. Then, **ask the person what they really want**. If it is your own anger, feel it, discharge it, and **ask yourself what you really want**. Identify what need is not being met or what you are not getting.

When anger is expressed in a healthy way, it does not hurt anyone else or us. You can use the energy of anger to empower yourself to ask for what you really want. You can use the energy to protect yourself by setting boundaries.

Before being able to coherently state what you want, you may have to discharge the anger. Discharging anger can be done in many ways. First, breathe and tell yourself it is okay to feel the anger. Next, with an **intention** to release the anger, **do something physical**.

Exercises: **Discharge Anger**

- Shout out the anger or scream into a pillow;
- Scream inside your car as you drive down the freeway with music blasting;
- Vent it out with a friend or a therapist;
- Beat a pillow or use baton clubs;
- Walk or jog it out, dance it out, exercise it out;
- Clean your house (vacuum, scrub a toilet, sink or pots 'n pans);
- Throw rocks against rocks;
- Pull weeds in your garden; or anything else you can think of to get the anger moving and releasing.

Once the anger starts moving, feel the hurt, frustration or fear. Then, take a look at the thought you are holding that has scared and hurt you. Do you believe you are not capable, not good enough, or unlovable? Are you willing to ask for what you want?

I used to get hurt and angry when my current husband would not listen to me. I would isolate myself and feel unloved, unimportant, and scared that he would leave me. I would hold the anger in until it would erupt over something insignificant like him not picking up his dirty socks. My reaction would be out of proportion to the situation.

I had to learn how to move my anger at the time I was

feeling it. It took some time to even identify that I was having a feeling because my anger was shut down. I would notice my throat tight or a knot in my stomach. I told myself it was okay to feel anger. When I allowed myself to feel it, I would then do something physical like going for a walk in order to discharge it. I would tell myself that he does love me and that he is not going to leave me just because he was too busy or distracted to listen to me at that moment.

After, I had discharged the anger, I was able to go to him and ask him to listen to me. I shared my fears. He gave me reassurance, and we felt closer to each other, more intimate. He told me to ask him in the future if this was a good time to talk, and could he give me his attention. I agreed to do so, and he agreed to listen.

SADNESS

What do you do when you feel sad, hurt or are grieving? Apply the same steps as when you are experiencing fear. **Breathe** and allow yourself to **feel** it. Tell yourself it is okay to feel whatever it is you are feeling. Allow the emotion to move through you with your breath. Allow tears to flow. If your chest hurts or your throat tightens, breathe into it and allow the breath and the feeling. Tell yourself that you are okay and that you can handle this.

Most of us are afraid we will drown in the grief and never stop crying. Most men were raised to think it is not okay to cry, admit they are hurt or express their sadness. The pain is held in. Our culture is not comfortable with expressing grief. With most emotions, we do everything we can to distract ourselves from feeling our pain. We watch TV, surf the Internet, shop, eat, use drugs and alcohol, overwork, use other people to distract us by focusing on them, or even become compulsive exercisers.

It takes conscious intention and willingness to allow the feelings to be felt and let them move through us. Do not hold onto the pain. Let go. Allow your own grieving process. You may cry for a while. Then, it will stop and you may cry again seeing a Hallmark card commercial. Allow the tears to flow.

Grief has its own process, and it is different for everyone. When you experience a loss from death, illness, divorce, the end of a job, or a move, you may experience grief. It is a process that has five stages: shock, denial, anger, sadness and acceptance. The process may be short or long. It takes as long as it takes. It is important to allow the process. Allow the feelings to be felt, and the emotional energy will flow through you.

You can access your sadness if you want to release it. Watch a sad movie, and allow the tears. Listen to emotive music. Read a story that is heartfelt. Put yourself in a bath or jump into the ocean or a lake. Water is the element of emotion and will assist in emotions moving and releasing.

GUILT/SHAME

What do you do when you experience guilt and shame? Most of us push it down. It just feels too bad to feel the guilt and awful to feel ashamed. Again, guilt and shame need to be felt. **Allow the feeling**. Do not push it down or hold it in. *Guilt* comes from making yourself wrong for *what you have done*. *Shame* comes from feeling you are wrong for simply *being* how you are. The hurt can run deep and is a result of judgments you are holding.

Let go of guilt by stopping the judgment from yourself and from others. Stop thoughts that make you wrong for being or thinking differently. The release of guilt and shame occur when you **accept yourself**, and your experiences with compassion and understanding.

When I was growing up, I felt ashamed for being racially mixed, for being a human with needs, and for being sexual. I blamed myself for being sexually molested. I thought something was wrong with me. I thought I was bad for being cute, and it was my fault that the molestation happened. I held the shame in my sexual organs and I had a lot of health problems related to my reproductive system (vaginal infections, endometriosis, pelvic inflammatory disease and infertility).

Through awareness, healings and the release of the shame and guilt I have come to accept myself as a human being with needs, including sexual needs. I was able to accept that as a child I was not wrong or responsible and did not deserve what happened to me. From my child's mind, I did not understand that it was not sex; it was abuse. I also believed that I was bad for having sex outside marriage.

There were so many rules of behavior in my religion that said a girl or women need to be and act a certain way. I believed I was wrong a lot of the time, a sinner. I was riddled with guilt when I went against my parents' wishes, the church or even the culture. I stopped myself from doing what felt right for me because I thought it was wrong based on someone else's definition of right and wrong.

My older brother told me it was a waste of time to feel guilty. I wasted so much time feeling guilty. At one point, I decided not to feel guilty by not going against the rules. However, that did not work because some of the rules did not feel right for me. After my near-death experience, I started listening to what felt right and began acting upon it. If I felt guilty, I would ask myself what was right for me. I would let go of the guilt, stop doing what was not right for me and do what I wanted to do.

I released the shame of being different (racially mixed and a sexual being who is tall) and have now come to accept and feel pride for the racial and cultural heritage that I am and have experienced. I accept that I am different and I am okay!

DARK NIGHT OF THE SOUL

*"Faith is a gift of the spirit that allows the soul
to remain attached to its own unfolding."*
Thomas Moore

In the mystical tradition, the dark night of the soul seems an inevitable part of the journey for those on a spiritual path. The dark night is a long journey into despair, hopelessness, loss of faith and a general shaking up of your foundational belief system. You deeply question your life, beliefs, and purpose. You must pass through this place of "initiation" in order to know yourself fully. You may have a sense of losing yourself or how you have defined yourself, your self-image. You are never the same when you come out the other side. However long it takes, the good news is that you do come out. The image you have of yourself must fall away in order for your true authentic self to emerge.

Faith, believing with out visible proof, is usually

restored when doing activities that center you like being out in nature, meditating, and reading inspiring materials, or being creative. It is also helpful to be with people who see who you truly are and can help you remember the wisdom of your Spirit. They can give you the encouragement to make it through.

The dark night descended upon me slowly like smoke filling a room from a fireplace not vented. You do not see it until your eyes are burning and you are choking. It crept up on me gradually, over a few months.

I left Maui, Hawaii where I had been living for two years to go on an adventure into the Four Corners area of the Southwest to explore the ancient Anasazi Indian ruins at Mesa Verde and Chaco Canyon.

It took a lot to get me off Maui. What got me to leave Maui came in a disguise and the convenience of exploring a love relationship with a man I had met on Maui, but who lived in Colorado. We were having a long distance affair, and I felt it was time to spend more time together to see how we got along on a daily basis. I felt drawn to the Four Corners area, and he was up for the adventure of camping and touring. So, off we went. I did not realize until later that I was really on a spiritual quest.

When I began my adventure into the Four Corners, obsession filled me. I went from ruin to ruin not quite knowing why or what I was looking for. Every ruin we came upon sent me into an altered state of consciousness.

I felt transported back in time living the life of these ancient peoples. One evening when the moon was full I joined a group of women for a ceremony in a *kiva* (a round place below ground used by the Anasazi for ceremony) in Aztec, New Mexico. During the drumming, I felt spirits all around me and experienced myself as an ancient wise woman who gave healing and information on the tribe's history. It was a time of remembering.

I remember having been exiled from the tribe when another group came and took over. As a wise woman, I had felt the Earth was always there to nourish and protect me, but I died in the desert that lifetime. I discovered I had been holding a fear of the desert in my present life and resentment against the Earth for having forsaken me. During this ceremony of remembering, I understood why I had to come back to these desert dwellings. I experienced forgiveness toward the Earth and released long held fear.

Guided by Spirit to do a vision quest, I took off by myself going deeper into the desert to further understand and know my purpose. It was time to continue healing my relationship with the Earth. I remembered that the Earth does heal and nourish, but it also destroys. Fear of the destructive power need not keep one from receiving the nourishment and beauty the Earth has to offer. I experienced love for the Earth and accepted her as my home.

The vision quest was also to heal my relationship with my spiritual master teacher, Jesus Christ. I had been raised Christian, but was no longer identifying myself as such. As a child of three-years-old, I had experienced Jesus and two Archangels, Michael and Gabriel standing at the foot of my bed. They would talk to me and answer my questions. Mostly, I felt loved and protected by them. My father did not believe me when I shared my experiences and would tell me I had to wait until I died and went to heaven to talk to Jesus. I did not believe him and kept talking to Jesus.

The condemning, hell, fire and brimstone God, who supposedly loved you if you were good enough and if you repented your sins, which were covered in the blood of Jesus, did not make sense to me. Christians who would kill in the name of Jesus, take people's land and enslave them caused me great sorrow and confusion. I rejected this condemning and punishing God in my late teens and rejected Jesus as well. I did not want to be that kind of Christian.

To say the least, I was rather surprised when Jesus Christ showed up in the desert and began talking to me as he did when I was a child. I knew him right away and experienced him as an iridescent light in the shape of a person. I recognized the eyes with a soft loving feeling that shined forth from the light form. The voice seemed familiar in a gentle kind way. I felt a lot of resistance to him telling me he was here to work with me. I got angry and stubbornly began to question what was really going on with the so-called Christians. I let him know I did not want to be one of "them."

He told me that his teachings were not being followed, and for me not to throw everything out or put everyone in the same category, essentially to let of go my judgment of Christians. I was shown what had happened to the early Christians who had lost their lives in accepting a new form of Judaism. The teachings are that God is within us and in all things, we are to love ourselves and love others as ourselves, we are to love our enemies and forgive those that hurt us, and to see God, Christ in everyone.

Jesus Christ asked me to open my heart with love and forgiveness and see the good in his teachings, not just what power-hungry scared men do to control others. He asked me to accept him again as my teacher. He asked that I see him as me for he is One with me. He told me that he was here to assist me in the healing work I was doing. I was reminded of the child-like trust and love that I had once experienced. He let me know that he and the angels were still with me and had been with me all my life and now was the time to ask consciously for their guidance and assistance. I felt his love move through me erasing my fear.

There were many fears from the past, fear of dying and being tortured for being a Christian, and the fear of being misunderstood. These were fears from another life that I still carried in my Soul. Now, here in the desert, it was time for me to heal from the pain of my many past lives. My purpose in coming to the desert was also to heal and re-establish my relationship with Christ and begin to trust again.

After the vision quest, I went back to the trailer I was staying in and found a message on the answering machine from two good friends I knew on Maui. One friend had returned to her home in Washington state, leaving Maui shortly after I had. The other friend was visiting her. They asked me to come and be part of an intentional spiritual community that was forming around a man who was "channeling" Jesus. A *channel* brings the energy or communication of another person through themselves. The community's intention was to live in harmony with the land and use solar energy, grow organic food and be self-sufficient. It fit into old dreams I had of living off the land in harmony with the Earth like the tribes of ancient times. I felt drawn to be a part of it.

Strangely enough I received a message from Christ while in the desert that it was time for me to leave Colorado. During the vision quest, I also knew that the relationship with the man I was involved with was not what I wanted. I was ready to move on, but needed confirmation from my Inner Guidance as to the best place for me to go. I was open to going back to Maui and had even considered moving back home to Minnesota. A quick answer of "no" to Minnesota and "no" to Maui was received. I got a "yes" to Washington, I packed up and was off to be a part of this spiritual community and to further my relationship with Jesus Christ.

While living in Tacoma, Washington I fully entered the dark night. The fears and doubts I had in the desert were nothing compared to the abyss I sank into in Washington. Nothing seemed to work for me anymore. All the things I had been taught and was teaching did not feel true or real for me. My Inner Guidance stopped. I was not getting any clear messages. I stopped working and was barely surviving. I was scared!

I felt alone and disconnected and could not get my grounding or a sense of being centered. Christ was not communicating with me nor were the angels. I would go to the man "channeling" Jesus for answers. I had lost my trust in myself and began to give my power over to the *channel*. Then, I began to question that form of communication. I wanted it directly from Source! Why wasn't I getting it?

Nothing made sense to me and I did not know what I was doing. I could not get any clients for healings or counseling work. I was totally disillusioned with being part of a spiritual community where everyone wanted someone else to do the work of living in harmony with the land, yet no one was willing to give up control, including me. I was ready to stop everything. In fact, I did. I stopped going to the person "channeling." I stopped being part of this so-called communit, and I stopped looking for healing work. I withdrew into my room and sat in the darkness feeling afraid and alone.

Sitting in my room, I heard a basketball bouncing

incessantly in the park across the street. It struck my last nerve. I remembered my older brother had a *basketball Jones* (obsession), and played from morning to night. It was his passion, but it drove me crazy. I felt as if I had descended into hell as the ball bounced again and again.

What did I do to have deserved this punishment? I had followed Inner Guidance and come to Washington to be part of this developing spiritual community. I did not feel I belonged there. I had no healing or counseling work, and my money was running out fast. I could not help anyone because I could not help myself.

I was staying in one the community members' home and essentially was being taken care of by her. Even though I had a place to stay and food to eat, I just could not seem to get anything going. I doubted myself and wondered if I had mistaken the guidance to move here. Did I really want to be part of a community living off the land? No! That was an old fantasy. I wanted to be in the world contributing. Then, why was I really here?

I took a job as a waitress in an upscale Italian restaurant. I like good food and felt that this was a way to be of service in the world and feed myself too. I kept holding the vision of being of service as part of my purpose, even though I was questioning how to be of service. Maybe it was time for me to stop doing healing work. How could I help anyone when I was depressed? I doubted that I knew anything and surely could not even help myself or anyone else in the dark emotional state I was experiencing.   If this dive into poverty, depression and uncertainty was life following Spirit, then I did not want to live, not this way.

Two months passed being in the dark night and eking out a survival existence. Fun or joy seemed elusive and I remembered a time not too long before when I had experienced joy. What had happened to me? Knowing that in the past I always felt better out in nature, I struck out on a hike up Mount Rainier. After all, I could always jump from the mountaintop and end my misery.

What I found on the mountaintop was inspiration and perspective. After the long arduous trek up, I reached a ridge with a panoramic view of Mount Hood, Mount Baker and the summit of Mount Rainier. I shouted out to God angrily. I called on Jesus. I demanded my life to change from survival to abundant living. I screamed to know what I was doing here in Washington. I demanded answers.   Furiously and breathlessly I shook my fist upward.

A cool breeze caressed my face and calm descended upon me. My breathing softened and moved gently. Something in me surrendered. I surrendered to the spiritual aspect of myself that was wiser and more knowing. I was willing to trust that part of me even though I did not understand it with my mind. I felt deep inside that it was beyond my mind to grasp what God was or even why I was. I simply was. I did exist. I saw there was much to learn. I saw clearly that my lesson was to trust myself and allow myself to receive inner support and guidance. It was time to stop looking outside myself for the answers from a channeler or even a spiritual teacher.

The dark night was a test of my faith in Spirit and myself. Everything around me seemed to take on a surrealist glow. Colors were brighter. Everything looked clear and the details of the rocks and trees jumped out with definition. I felt strong, warm and vibrantly full of energy.

Surrendering means to let go and trust. Let go the control and trust. Just as the trapeze artist flies through the air swinging from the trapeze by letting go of the bar and flying for a few seconds before grabbing the next bar. In those few seconds, the flier has to trust as she reaches out. Many times in our lives, we have to let go of the old. We often must surrender the thoughts that scare us. We must stop trying to hold on to limiting thoughts that do not serve or empower us and reach out for something new. It requires letting go of the familiar and trusting—changing—growing.

Getting mad at God works. Discharging the anger and fear helped me get the clarity I needed. I could not be clear if I was afraid or bursting with anger. After the explosion of anger, I saw that I had to let go of the beliefs that I was not worthy to have money or support or guidance, especially the guidance of Christ or the angels.

∽SPIRITUAL PRINCIPLE∽
Let It Be Easy. Let Go of the Struggle.

I had been used to being in struggle my whole life. I grew up believing life is hard, that life is a struggle. I was dismantling beliefs and images of who I thought I was and what I thought I needed. Was I worthy enough to receive money? I always compared myself to others, and I usually came up feeling inferior. I felt inadequate and undeserving. I needed to discover my inner qualities of value, worth, love, compassion, acceptance, faith, trust, wisdom and perseverance. It was time for me to own and claim myself, my new authentic self, and release the old self from my past programming, to no longer be limited by my past!

~SPIRITUAL PRINCIPLE~
Your History is not Your Destiny.

"You can rise above your rais'in," says Oprah Winfrey. Your past does not have to define your future. You no longer need to be limited by your past, as you claim your power to create in the present.

As the light broke through the darkness and shone in my consciousness, I began letting go of the image that I had to look good, and be there for others and deny what I wanted. The myth that the guru had the answers for me was blown apart. I found the answers were within me now. I was in the process of facing my fear of global catastrophe and Earth changes. No longer could I run away to some "safe" place and live there in peace by shutting out the world. I realized it was not about a place out there, but a place inside me where peace resides.

This awareness and these insights flashed through me in seconds as if stuck by a thunderbolt of heavenly gossamer fairy dust. However, it took months for it all to integrate and make sense to my left brain logical, analytical mind. But for now, the fight with myself and with God had ended. I felt peaceful and uplifted. Trusting Spirit, I surrendered to whatever lay ahead of me. The sun shone brightly. The dark night was over.

Back into Life

I went back to the restaurant the next day to work and simply enjoyed myself with the customers, and, of course, eating the fettucine alfredo with prawns. Miraculously, the basketball stopped bouncing outside my bedroom window. Maybe the kids left for camp, moved away from the neighborhood or I went deaf. It was strange because I do not remember hearing the ball bounce anymore. I had ascended out of hell and came back into life. I had let go of the struggle in my mind. Did I have more money? No. My needs, however, were provided for. I was receiving from many sources. I had food, a free place to live and hope that I could contribute once again.

Shortly after taking the journey up the mountain, I met a woman who did massage therapy. We talked and I told her of the healing work I had previously done in other states and my desire to practice here. She referred a man to me for a healing. He came to see me. I felt insecure because I had not worked for several months, and hoped that my intuition would work once again. During the dark night, I could not sense, see or know anything about anyone, anything or myself.

In a small hallway between bedrooms, I set up two chairs and my massage table. Settling in, I grounded and centered myself and gave him my full attention. He had been diagnosed as having an aneurysm in his brain that was about to burst threatening his life. He was scheduled for surgery, but he did not want to go under the knife. So, taking a chance he walked out of his doctors' office. Now, he was in front of me hoping for a miracle.

Placing my hands on his head after I had scanned his body and had done some clearing of his electro-magnetic field, I sensed a pressure and heat. I felt that he was very angry, that he had been betrayed and was suffering a great loss regarding his land. The anger and pressure had built up in his head. As I was channeling energy and focusing on love and well being for him he began to talk, then cry. The pressure lessened and the heat subsided.

At the end of the session, he expressed feeling relieved and at peace about the situation and was not afraid of the aneurysm bursting. He requested that I come to his home in Gig Harbor, about forty minutes from where I was staying and work on him again and also on his wife. I agreed.

When I arrived at his home a few days later, he reported the good news from his doctor. It appeared the aneurysm had disappeared. They thought the CAT scan had made a mistake. He attributed the change to the healing he had received. He wanted another energy healing to make sure all was well and to do more emotional work. He wanted to forgive the county that was taking his land.

Then surprisingly, he offered me a cottage to live in on their twenty-five acre property with a blackberry hedged pond where eagles flew, an orchard where deer nibbled the apples at dawn. There was a hill to climb to watch the sunset over Puget Sound where the colors reflected in the water. He and his wife were going to Mexico for six months before their land was to be sold. Even though they had a caretaker, they wanted me on the property doing healing work as a way to thank me. They paid me money for the healing too. What a gift! They also offered me the use of a car. It was a good thing too as mine had blown it's engine, and I desperately needed a car.

I gratefully accepted with full awareness that the Universe was taking care of me, and this was my opportunity to fully receive and know it was finally okay to allow abundance into my life. Some lazy afternoons, after doing a few healings, I took walks to Puget Sound where the sea breezes blew and the sea gulls flew, and allowed myself to reflect on my good fortune. Cherie Carter-Scott defines this as a state of grace, "To live in a state of grace means to be fully in tune with your Spiritual nature and a higher power that sustains you...you trust in yourself and the Universe."

Another amazing opportunity came soon after the dark night ended. Once again I was offered work as the healing practitioner and co-facilitator at retreats conducted in Hawaii by Alan Cohen. I left my sanctuary on this secluded property in Washington several times to go back to my spiritual home in Hawaii to work. The work and being in Hawaii brought me great joy.

I was being supported at many levels and was asked to resume traveling to other cities to teach and do healings. Although I had traveled before, it escalated at this time. I was out in the world again contributing with much greater trust and sense of myself.

I was guided once again to move, this time to Santa Barbara, California. Spirit assured me that my healing work would expand, and I would meet my life mate partner. I once again trusted and made the move. Now, my life is filled with a loving husband and healing work that supports and fulfills me.

INTENTION

"Intention and desire in the field of pure
potentiality have infinite organizing power."
Deepak Chopra

An intention is an affirmation or statement. Setting an intention means to identify a goal by stating what you want to create and experience based on what your heart desires. In order to know what you want or desire, first center yourself, then ask within to know what is in your heart. What is it you truly want? You may discover beliefs that say you cannot have what you want. You may not feel deserving or worthy to have what you want. Releasing these beliefs will take some work with your Spiritual Self and maybe even a therapist, counselor or healer to help you in releasing those beliefs that limit you from experiencing your hearts' desires.

Setting Intentions

Statements of intentions need to be positive and in the present. They are affirmations that include statements like:

> "I am"
> "I have"
> "I experience"
> "I create"
> "I receive"
> "I accept"

~SPIRITUAL PRINCIPLE~
***Energy Follows Thought and Thought
with Emotion Creates.***

What we hold in our thoughts and with our emotions, desires or feelings is what we create, whether it is something we want or do not want. If you want a red sports car and you visualize yourself driving it and how it makes you feel, you can manifest owning a red sports car. If you fear getting a raise and worry about it and see your bills piling up, you will not get the raise.

We are thinking and affirming all the time, be it positive or negative. Stating an intention focuses our thoughts on what we want to create or experience. Most of the time our thoughts or affirmations are negative, judgmental and limiting. Thoughts such as: "I cannot have or be," "I am stupid," "I do not deserve," "I am not good enough," and "I do not have enough time or money."

When we consciously change our thinking by creating positive affirmations (intentions) and then plan our action steps, we are aligning our thoughts with positive emotions (feelings) to achieve what we want to create.

Examples of an intentions:

"My intention is that I am grounded and centered in all that I do. I live my life from a grounded and centered place."

Action Steps: I take action to create the experience of being grounded and being centered by:

1. Breathing and connecting to the Earth before I do anything physical and when I am with another person;
2. Moving my awareness into my *center* by thinking and visualizing myself centered in love or peace or in a golden sphere of light that represents my Spiritual Self.

"I intend to be open to receive."

Action Step: When someone gives me a compliment, the action I take is to take a breath and consciously allow the feeling in.

After setting intentions, create action steps that you can do to bring your intention into form or reality. The intention to receive may include receiving love, a relationship, money, abundance, a new job, home or whatever you desire. You may want to take an action by visualizing yourself like a flower opening to the sun or an open tube with water flowing through to represent your openness to receive. Visualize yourself receiving or experiencing whatever it is you want to create, enjoy, or experience.

Holding a thought or intention such as "I am peace" or "I am love" brings that vibration of peace or love into your consciousness and into your life experience. When stating intentions, they need to be positive, in present time, and active. They need to have a feeling attached to the thought.

Examples of Other Intentions:

"With each breath I take I am grounded and centered."

"Each day I experience more joy in my life."

"Today I am experiencing love and acceptance in my relationship with my spouse."

"Now I am open and receiving my life mate."

"Money is coming to me from many sources and I am now open to receiving it."

Most of us need to be diligent in observing our thoughts and stop the inner dialogue that scares us, limits us and sabotages us. Once you bring your awareness to what you are thinking, you can change the program by changing the thought. Think new thoughts. Put your attention on new thoughts. Awareness is the first step. Change the thought by setting an intention to do so. **"I now change the negative thoughts that scare me easily and I put my attention on thoughts that uplift me and empower me."**

～SPIRITUAL PRINCIPLE～
What You Put Your Attention on Grows.

If you think, "I am fat," you get fatter. If you think, "I am poor," you have lack of money. Change the thought with a new thought (intention) that uplifts, inspires, affirms and empowers you. Give it your attention. You get more of what you think about. Create yourself anew. Create the life you want to experience and enjoy. You have the power within you to change yourself and your life by changing your thinking about yourself and the world.

You get what you believe, not what you want. Wanting is defined as "desire unfulfilled." It is important to know what you want and what the desires are within your heart. It is important to know that you deserve to have what you want, and that you can have what you want.

I grew up believing I could not have what I wanted. As a result, I stopped wanting. If someone asked me what I wanted, I did not know. If someone asked what movie I wanted to see, I was so out of touch with my desires that I would say, "Whatever you want is okay for me."

It is essential to know what you want. Know the desires that lie within your heart. Know that you can have what you want. Spirit is not waiting until you are worthy enough to give you what you want. You can not earn your worth by "doing" or being "good." You already are worthy, valuable and deserving. Affirm **"I AM WORTHY AND DESERVING."**

⁓SPIRITUAL PRINCIPLE⁓
Like Attracts Like.

Everything is energy. Energy has vibration and frequency. Metaphysically, *like attracts like*. We are used to thinking that opposites attract. However, when two thoughts, emotions, or beliefs are the same, they attract. The thought sets up a vibration that acts like a magnet and draws to it another vibration of the same frequency.

If you believe or think life is hard, you will attract hard situations to yourself. If you think you are unlovable, you will attract people who are not being loving into your life. If you do not listen to yourself or lie to yourself, you will attract others into your life who will not listen to you or who will lie to you. If your thinking is fear-based, your experiences will be filled with fear. Change your thinking to uplifting and empowering thoughts. As you think, so are you.

Know this: You get what you believe, not what you want. Believe...know you are worthy. Let yourself know your wants and desires, but do not stay in the wanting. Remember: Wanting is desire unfulfilled. Stop staying in the want. Change your thought from wanting something to choosing it, to creating it, to experiencing it. State it as an intention and claim it now. See yourself already having it **now**! Move from the wanting to visioning and experiencing your heart's desires fulfilled now.

Creating What You Really Want in Your Life

After getting clear on your intentions and action steps, the next step is to **visualize and feel** yourself experiencing what you want to create and bring into your life. Manifestation or creation involves having a clear thought an intention combined with emotion. Visualize and feel it as if it is actually occurring in the now, this present moment. Then, let go of attachment to how or when it will manifest.

It is like placing an order at a restaurant. You are hungry for shrimp capellini. You visualize yourself eating it, smelling it and tasting it. Feel how satisfied you will be experiencing the food. Then you order it and wait. Now, you are not sure how this restaurant is going to prepare it. You know that sauces differ at restaurants. The pasta could be freshly made or not. You trust that you will get what you ordered.

It is the same process as when you place an order with the Universe. Wait and trust. Hold the vision. Feel the experience of receiving what your heart desires.

During my meditation New Year's morning of 1993, I set an intention to have a committed, monogamous relationship with my life partner. I then affirmed and visualized twice a day in meditation: "My life partner is with me now sharing my life in a harmoniously loving, committed and monogamous relationship. We experience love, joy and fun together." I saw and felt myself experiencing love, joy and doing fun things together. Six weeks later he came into my life. This is exactly what I created and am now experiencing with my husband Joe.

Before meeting my current husband, I had numerous failed relationships. I used to believe that I did not deserve to be loved, because I was not worthy enough for a man to love and be committed to me. In the past, I also believed that men were not trustworthy. I had to change these beliefs in order to change my experience.

I learned that the most important person to trust was myself. I now trust my ability to discern what is really going on beyond appearances. I can now see who is trustworthy. I learned how to love and value myself and came to know that I am lovable and deserving of love. I am still learning how to love and accept myself more each day. It takes a lot of work and self-awareness to change the old program, but now I am experiencing a healthy, happy, loving relationship with myself and with my husband.

INTENTION IS POWERFUL!

COMPASSION, LOVE AND FORGIVENESS

"There is nothing in this world
that cannot be healed by forgiveness."
Alan Cohen

When we are centered in our Spiritual Self, we are centered in the compassion and love that we are as spiritual beings. Most of us do not stay in a centered state and allow fear and emotional pain to separate us from others and from ourselves. What we need is to return to love. By the very process of centering we return to the love that is within us and the love that we are. Our hearts contain love and compassion. This is an experience of fullness, overflowing, warmth, expansiveness and inclusiveness.

However, the heart may be closed down from holding onto past hurts, disappointments, resentments, anger, guilt and shame. These are the blocks to love. When the heart is filled with pain, you cannot feel the love, joy, peace or compassion that is within it. Healing of the heart may need to occur in order to feel centered in love. Healing occurs from forgiving yourself or others. Forgiveness occurs when you allow yourself to experience, to feel the emotions that have been suppressed, repressed and shut down.

One cannot rush to forgive. You need to allow yourself to feel the pain of what hurt you. The emotional energy needs to flow through the heart to clear the way for love and compassion to be felt. What was blocked or held in needs to be released.

Forgiveness is for the self, not necessarily for the person that caused harm to you. Forgiveness frees the self to fully feel and express and get on with life. Holding onto pain only continues to hurt you.

Qualities of Forgiveness:
Acceptance, *Compassion*, and *Understanding*

Forgiveness is a process of giving forth compassion, acceptance and when possible understanding. Sometimes it is not possible to understand what happened to you or to others. In those cases, you need to let go of the need to understand. See yourself and others with compassion, as doing the best they or you could do. See them or yourself as scared or afraid. You know what it feels like to be scared and to not know what to do. Have you experienced trying to do your best yet feeling lost or confused?

Accept what you "did" or "did not do" that caused hurt based on what you knew to do at the time. Those that have hurt you "did" or "did not do" what hurt you based on what they knew to do at the time.

There are several definitions of acceptance. I am not using accept to mean approval or to receive. Acceptance means to reconcile oneself to a situation. Accept that it happened. Accept yourself without judgment.

Remember: One way we learn is by making mistakes. Most of the time it is easier to forgive others than to forgive yourself. You can be your own worst enemy with judgments, condemnations and punishments. You blame yourself for making mistakes when you were doing the best you could at the time based on what you knew at the time. Forgive yourself for thinking you ever did anything wrong. Stop the thoughts of judgment. Stop making yourself wrong. Stop hurting yourself.

If you have ever blamed yourself, judged or criticized yourself, made yourself wrong and felt guilty, then do this exercise: Write as many times as you need, "With regard to _____, I forgive myself for ever thinking I was wrong." (Recommended by author Iyanla Vanzant)

Example: With regard to the molestation I experienced between the ages of eight and nine by my male, teenage baby-sitter, I forgive myself for ever thinking I was wrong—that it was my fault. I was innocent. I was a child. I was abused. There was nothing wrong with me.

~SPIRITUAL PRINCIPLE~
Forgiveness Heals.

Forgiveness means you are willing to let go of the hurt. It does not mean that you were not hurt. Judgments and criticisms hurt, as does betrayal, abandonment and shame. Forgiveness acknowledges the hurt, but says I am letting this hurt go because I care for myself. I am willing to stop hurting myself by holding onto this pain. Forgiveness releases the pain you hold.

One day a beautiful, well-dressed woman came to me for a healing. She told me she wanted to forgive her father. She was in her early forties and had been holding anger toward him since she was a child. As the story unfolded, she told me her father had killed her mother and stabbed her twice in the heart area as she sat in her highchair. He also stabbed her brother. She was only about eighteen months old and her brother was two years older than she was. After attacking his children, he killed himself. She and her brother survived. She continually felt pain in her heart into adulthood even though the physical wounds were long healed.

I asked her, "Are you ready to forgive your father?" She said, "Yes. I want to be pain free and anger free." We began the process of letting go the hurt and anger. She opened her heart to feel compassion for her father who was in such deep pain and fear that he would strike out and try to kill his loved ones and end up killing himself. As the tears flowed, she spoke to her father's spirit with love, "Thank you for giving me my life."

She indeed has had a wonderful life with adopted parents who love her. She is very successful in her career and has a loving husband. The pain in her heart left as she opened her heart to forgiveness.

NON-JUDGMENT

"A day spent judging another is a painful day.
A day spent judging yourself is a painful day.
You don't have to believe your judgments;
they're simply an old habit."
The Buddha

Non-judgment is being neutral. It is being in acceptance of what is. The rose does not consider itself more or less beautiful than an orchid or an oak tree. It has no judgment. It does not compare. It does not say, "I am good and you are bad." The full moon is no less beautiful than the new moon. The tide flows in and out. One is not better than the other. Nature shows us that variety and diversity exists. Nature is without judgment. It simply is.

Most humans are judgmental. We do not accept others or ourselves as we are. We tend to place ourselves above or below someone. We tend to make one experience better than or less than another. We are constantly judging. We think in terms of good or bad.

When I was on retreat with a group during a Therapeutic Touch healing training we were instructed to be aware of how much we judged. Every time we judged ourselves, another, or a situation we were to raise our hand. My hand was continually shooting up into the air. After the first hour, I found myself resting my hand on top of my head as judgments passed through my mind rapidly. I had known that I was critical of myself, but I had not realized how much judging I did. Judgments hurt. Becoming aware of the judgments helped me to stop the thoughts. Thereby, I learned to stop hurting myself. I came to accept the way I am. I am of mixed race. I look the way I look. I talk the way I talk. I write the way I write. I am okay the way I am.

It takes discipline to train the mind to think differently. Stop the critical thought and replace it with a thought that is neutral, accepting, positive and empowering.

Exercise: **Become Aware of Your Judgments**

1. Every time you have a judgment mentally or physically raise your hand or a finger.
2. **Stop the judgment.**
3. Tell yourself that you are okay, or that the other person is okay.
4. Tell yourself to accept what is. **"It is what it is."**
5. Make a list of your judgments then change them to neutral, accepting, positive and empowering statements.

6. See yourself, the other person, or the situation with compassion.

Human beings grow and thrive in an atmosphere of love and acceptance, praise and encouragement. Criticism and judgment makes us contract, fearful and defensive. It closes us off from learning.

~SPIRITUAL PRINCIPLE~
Life is Your Mirror.

Things that happen to us in our life act as a mirror by showing us something about ourselves. If we are judging someone it is usually something about ourselves that we do not like and the other person is mirroring it for us. Most of the time we do not consciously see it in ourselves, but we can easily see it in the other person. Carl Jung says, "Everything that irritates us about others can lead us to an understanding of ourselves."

Life situations also show us what we believe. Remember: We create from what we believe. Our beliefs are held in our subconscious. Life will bring our subconscious beliefs to our consciousness. Life is a mirror.

A single mother in her early forties came to me for a healing session because her life was full of struggle. She was constantly anxious and fearful and on the edge financially, barely making it from month to month. We began to look at her life and what her life was mirroring to her. We looked at her beliefs. She believed life was hard and a struggle, and that there was not enough money, time or love. She also believed she was not good enough no matter how hard she worked, and that she was not worthy of love. These beliefs kept her in a state of fear that she would not get what she needed whether it was love, money or ease in her life.

In order to change her life, she needed to change her beliefs. She worked with her Spiritual Self in releasing the beliefs that kept her in fear and chose to look at life as easy and herself as lovable and capable. She began affirming that she was enough and had enough and looked to her Spirit to guide her. Remarkably, her life began to change to reflect her new beliefs.

As a healing practitioner, it is imperative to be accepting and not be judgmental. I may not see the big picture of what someone is experiencing or learning. I may not know all of what someone is going through. Healing can happen on a physical, emotional, mental or spiritual level. If I were to judge the experience as bad or wrong, it would take away the value the experience has to offer for that person growth. Remember the spiritual principle: *Everything Serves.*

All things work together for "good." Realize you may not see the whole picture and what the outcome will be.

See the positive, the blessing, the gift in all things. Everything we experience serves us and adds to our growth. Realize that you may not see what lies ahead. Trust that it will all work out.

There is a story of a young man who became a cripple from falling off his horse. His father, a wealthy king who ruled over vast lands, heard his servants exclaim, "How awful. This is a terrible thing that has happened to the prince." The father said with acceptance, "It is what it is."

While the prince was recovering, there was a drought and the crops died. The people exclaimed, "How awful. This is the worst thing that could happen." The king said calmly, "It is what it is."

During the drought the land was over run by warriors from another kingdom. The subjects were again in distress exclaiming, "How awful. This is so bad. What are we to do?" The king said with acceptance, "It is what it is." Yet, there were no riches or foodstuffs for the invader to take.

So, the invaders decided to take slaves. As they were rounding up people to take as slaves, they came upon the prince. However, they did not take him because he was not an able-bodied man. Once again, the king with gratitude and acceptance said, "It is what it is."

∽SPIRITUAL PRINCIPLE∽
Accept what Is.

"Accepting a thing does not mean you approve of what is going on. Nor does it mean you are not being impacted by what is going on. Acceptance is knowing that no matter what, everything is and will be just fine." says author Iyanla Vanzant.

When you judge yourself, someone else, or a situation, you are closing your heart. See yourself, the person or situation with acceptance and compassion. Let go comparing yourself to someone else. Do not make yourself less than or greater than someone. You are unique.

Brugh Joy, a healer and author of *Joy's Way*, writes, "Make no comparisons. Make no judgments. Delete your need to understand. All three injunctions have to do with giving up ideas of what ought to be and accepting what is, and it is from hanging on to what ought to be and rejecting what is that pain comes."

In letting go the need to understand, realize you may not understand the bigger picture of what you or someone else is going through. You may not be able to figure out something that is beyond linear thinking in the realm of Spirit. Keep an open mind.

Being non-judgmental does not mean you are not discerning. The dictionary defines discernment as the ability to perceive by sight or some other sense, to recognize or distinguish. When something feels okay for you to do or not do, then go with your feeling. It is important to listen to the messages within you without judging them as good or bad.

NON-ATTACHMENT

"Learn to let go. That is the key to happiness."
The Buddha

Non-attachment simply means letting go and not holding on. It means being in the moment, not projecting into the future or reacting out from some past moment, whether that moment was fearful or joyful. Everything in life, everything we have, everything we experience is temporary. Our bodies are temporary. They do not last. They are constantly changing, moving from a state of health to illness to health, growing, aging, and dying. We only experience life for a short time. We attach to the body thinking this is I. Yet, we are so much more than the body.

The material possessions we have are here for us to enjoy in the moment for they too will break down, wear out, become obsolete. They are temporary. Our relationships are also temporary. Our mate will die, we will die, so will our children. Friends will come and go. Life in the body on this planet is temporary, impermanent.

We are forever wanting. Wanting more, wanting something new and different. Wanting something to end or to begin. Never satisfied. We do not experience the joy, comfort, the satisfaction or acknowledgment, or the peace of the moment. As one moment moves into the next, we hold on resisting the flow. Life is constantly changing, moving, shifting.

Yet, we hold on. We hold on fearful of change, fearful that letting go would leave us empty and alone. We attach to the pain or the joy of an experience, a thing, or a person. We hold on. We attach. We do not let go. We tend not to be present in the moment, but remember the past and try to recreate it. By jumping into the future with our thoughts, we expect or fear that the future will be the same or worse than what we have already experienced. We worry and become anxious. We are not in present time. The present is colored by our attachment to the past and our fear of the future. In the present moment, there is no fear.

~SPIRITUAL PRINCIPLE~
Let Go. Be Present.

Stop holding onto the pain. Stop holding onto the joy. Stop comparing that this experience is *less than* that experience or *greater than* that experience. Remember: **Accept what is**.

Letting Go

If you find that you are attached and holding on, then let go. Letting go is easier when you discover why you are holding on. It is important to ask yourself:

1. What do I get from holding on?
2. How does holding on serve me?
3. What would I experience if I let go?

Recently, I heard a story from a woman who told me she had trouble letting go of her relationship with her partner. Metaphorically, she held on so intensely that as she was leaving she left claw marks on him. During the counseling session we took a look at what she was holding onto. She felt he was the only one who could love her, even though this had not been a loving relationship. He was critical and abusive.

She saw that the relationship was serving her by teaching her to stop looking outside herself for love. This man was not the source of her love. She realized that the source of love was within her. In letting him go, she could now experience loving herself.

Non-attachment means letting go of expectations and outcomes. Non-attachment is simply being in acceptance of what is, letting go of expectations. Non-attachment is not holding on or trying to keep something or someone from changing, even if that someone is you.

As a healing practitioner, I have learned not to attach to what I think healing looks like. I learned to let go of expectations, and the need to understand and to make no judgments. Healing can take place at many levels: physical, emotional, mental and spiritual.

A family whose father was dying of cancer called me. The cancer had started in the bladder and spread throughout his body. The doctors had done all they could with surgery, chemotherapy and radiation, but nothing stopped the cancer. He had been referred to me for spiritual healing by his doctor.

I came to his home and felt that after the first session healing was occurring. At that time, I did not know at what level. I had to let go my picture of what healing should look like. I wanted him to be pain free and to recover, to live. I had to remind myself that maybe death was the healing, and that my role might be to assist him in making a peaceful transition.

This is what occurred during the healing process. After the first energy work session the pain stopped. He was able to stop the morphine drip and become more conscious. He allowed himself to feel his emotions. Then, he was able to look at his life and see how he had held resentment and anger that were literally consuming him.

He began to let go by accepting that he had these feelings, and he began to express them. He vented anger at unseen friends and family members and to me.

His daughter called me one day to say, "Dad is in his room shouting. He has never done this. Is he going crazy?" I told her, "This is a good thing for he is letting go of pent-up anger. Give him your acceptance and give him space to let it out." He learned to express his feelings to his family, not only anger, but love. This process of healing became a healing for the whole family. They were able to change their pattern of holding anger and not expressing feelings.

He was able to forgive himself. He made amends and asked for forgiveness from some relatives and associates. He connected with the spiritual part of himself and came into acceptance and peace. He was able to let go of the body in peace.

I experienced the healing occur at many levels. Although he died after working with me for six weeks, he made a peaceful transition. I also felt at peace. I had let go my attachment to what the healing had to be or how it should look. His family, he and I experienced a healing. We accepted what was, and held the intention that healing would occur. It did.

INTEGRITY

"To thine own self be true."
William Shakespeare

Do you put off doing what you intuitively know is best for you? Do you walk your talk? Are you in denial of some truth you feel or know? Do you speak the truth about how you feel and what you really want? Being in *integrity* means taking actions that are consistent with what is true for you on the inside. It is living from that place of knowing within you. Being in integrity is being true to yourself. As you become true to yourself, you will be truthful with others in your life, and act from a place of truth, of authenticity.

◦SPIRITUAL PRINCIPLE◦
Tell the Truth.

How do you know what is true for you or what is in your heart? Ask to know from your Spiritual Self, then listen for the answer. Ask for courage to speak and live your truth. Tell the truth about your feelings, your wants and needs to those you are in relationship with. Release the shame and do not hide. Be your authentic self.

It was a cold, dark night. The wind was howling outside as the rain beat against the windows. I felt as if something severe and strong was trying to get inside. The feeling was extremely uncomfortable. Attempting to feel safe, I snuggled into the down comforter as I was lying on the couch. I had the overwhelming sense that something wanted my attention. The something was not the storm outside. It was the storm inside me.

I wanted to know what was going on inside me. Why was I so uncomfortable? I asked my Spiritual Self to know what I needed in order to feel safe and at peace. The answer came, "Stop lying to yourself." I asked what was the lie? My Spiritual Self said, "It is time to tell the truth to yourself regarding what you really want and what is important to you in your intimate relationships."

I realized it was long past the time to leave a relationship that I knew was no longer good for me. I had been involved in a relationship with a man who could not commit to me, and I was settling for less than I wanted. I pretended to be okay with what was going on. In fact, I pretended that nothing was going on. I denied that I was unhappy. I also lied to myself that having someone some of the time was better than no man in my life and being lonely. Recognizing the lie did not feel good. I faced the truth. I wanted someone who was available and ready to commit to me.

∾ SPIRITUAL PRINCIPLE ∾
Do Not Settle for Less.

The message from my Spirit was, "Do not settle for less. Know that you can have your heart's desire fulfilled by allowing the form to change." I understood that I had to stop looking to this person, who could not commit to me and be my partner. He was not available for the type of relationship I wanted.

As the storm began to rage outside, I surrendered. The storm ceased inside of me as I committed to living my truth. I decided it was better to be honest with myself and be at peace with myself even if I was alone.

Being in *integrity* means to "act" on the outside consistent with what is on the inside. Your insides match your outsides. **Walk your talk.** Come from your heart. Speak and live your truth.

LOVING YOURSELF

*"I find that when we really love, accept
and approve of ourselves exactly as we are,
then everything in life works."*
Louise Hay

In the process of learning to love yourself and take care of yourself, it is important to know what you feel and need. It is necessary to accept that what you want and feel is important. You are as important as others. It has been a common belief to think that you are selfish if you take time for yourself. You do not have to be self-sacrificing in order to be loved, or to be worthy. It does not mean you are a bad or selfish person when you take care of yourself first instead of always being there for others and meeting their needs. When you take time for yourself to meet your needs or do the things you want to do, then you will have more to give since you have filled yourself up by giving to yourself first. Fill up! You cannot give from an empty well.

What gets in the way of you being loving to yourself? It may be that you are not valuing yourself by believing you are worthless or undeserving. The belief that you are worthless and undeserving of love or goodness is not true. Your value is not dependent on what you do. The truth is you are valuable and have worth simply because you exist.

Recently, I received this *e-mail message*:

A well-known speaker started off his seminar by holding up a $20 bill. in the room of 200, he asked, "Who would like this $20 bill? Hands started going up. He said, "I am going to give this $20 to one of you but first, let me do this." He proceeded to crumple the dollar bill up. He then asked, "Who still wants it?" Still the hands were up in the air. "Well," he replied, "What if I do this?" And he dropped it on the ground and started to grind it into the floor with his shoe. He picked it up, now all crumpled and dirty. "Now who still wants it?" Still hands went into the air. "My friends, you have all learned a very valuable lesson. No matter what I did to the money, you still wanted it because it did not decrease in value. It was still worth $20. Many times in our lives, we are dropped, crumpled, and ground into the dirt by the experiences we have, by the decisions we make and the circumstances that come our way. We feel as though we are worthless. But no matter what has happened or what will happen, you will never lose your value. You are special. You are unique. **Remember, You are valuable.** Do not forget it!

Exercises: **How to Love Yourself**

- Be kind and compassionate with yourself. This is being loving.

- Be accepting of yourself. This is being loving.

- Honor, respect and value yourself. This is being loving.

- Give yourself encouragement. This is being loving.

- Forgive yourself. This is being loving.

- Take care of yourself. This is being loving.

When you become busy and other-oriented, you need to find balance by listening to your Spiritual Self. It is by listening to yourself that you know what to give yourself. It is how you become aware of what you need and how to meet the need.

Meditation is one tool, a *spiritual practice*, to use to connect with and listen to you. It is a way to be with yourself in the still quietness. When we love someone we want to be with them and give them our attention. We want to meet their needs. Connect with your Inner Source and pay attention by listening. Spending time listening and giving to yourself is being loving. Meeting you own needs is being loving to yourself.

As you listen to yourself, you become aware of the pain, guilt, shame and judgments that keep you from accessing the love within you. There is so much inside you that is wanting and crying out to be embraced and loved. As your awareness of self expands, you will be given the opportunity to accept and embrace all aspects of yourself. You begin to know more of yourself as you listen deeply to what is within you.

Let go of the attachment to pain and patterns of thought and behavior that keep you from being loving. These patterns may have served you in the past, but do they now? In releasing these patterns you can move deeper into loving and accepting yourself.

Exercises: **Accepting yourself**

1. Look at yourself in the **mirror** and tell yourself, "I love you unconditionally right now." Do this exercise morning and evening for 30 days. Then, continue with the affirmation for another 30 days looking at your body naked.

2. Use this affirmation during your day whenever you become aware of criticizing yourself. "I accept myself as I am right now."

Spiritual Practices:

1. Connect to your Spiritual Self/Inner Source.
2. Take time to listen to yourself and be with yourself (meditate).
3. Stop judging, criticizing and putting yourself down. Stop Invalidating how you feel.
4. Allow your feelings to flow. Feel your feelings and breathe through them. Do not hold on, push down or distract yourself from your feelings.
5. Appreciate, accept and value yourself right where you, are as you are.
6. Forgive yourself.
7. Give yourself encouragement and acknowledgment.
8. Ask yourself what you want. Say "yes" to what you want, and "no" to what you do not want.
9. Stop putting everyone else's needs and wants before yours, and stop doing things you do not want to do.
10. Do the things you want (take a walk, read, take a bath, play music, paint, meditate, get a massage, and go out in nature).
11. Take care of yourself physically with exercise, good nutritious food and water. Get plenty of rest.
12. Choose healthy relationships.
13. Do work that you like.
14. Express your creativity.
15. Walk your talk, and speak your truth.

My greatest lesson in this life has been and still is learning to love. To live my highest potential is to love myself and to love others.

Gratitude

Most human beings tend to focus on the negative. We notice what is wrong with ourselves. We notice faults in others and are quick to point them out. We think what we do is not enough and what we have is not enough. We are always looking to do more and have more.

Do you take time out to appreciate what you have or how much you have learned and grown? Do you give acknowledgment and appreciation to yourself, your loved ones, your employees or co-workers?

~SPIRITUAL PRINCIPLE~
Gratitude Opens Your Heart.

I remember the response Oprah Winfrey received from many of her viewers after she encouraged her audience to keep a gratitude journal. Saran Ban Breathnach, author of *Simple Abundance* and a guest on Oprah's show, wrote and spoke about creating a gratitude journal. Using a gratitude journal is simply writing down the things in each day (at least five things) that you are grateful for experiencing or having.

Examples:
1. I am grateful for my health.
2. I am grateful for getting the wash done.
3. I am grateful for the sun shining.
4. I am grateful the children are asleep.
5. I am grateful for my loving husband.

The audience response was similar to mine. Lives changed. There was more **joy** and **peace** and **love** in our hearts. The criticisms lessened. Greater intimacy and closeness was experienced. Priorities shifted. My focus shifted from "not enough" to I have so much abundance in my life and I have so much to appreciate. I began to acknowledge all that I do, and it is remarkable.

Being grateful assists in the manifestation process (the process of creating what you want to experience). Focusing on what you have gives you more. Remember: *Energy follows thought and thought with emotion creates.* Being grateful and appreciative brings peace to your mind, peace to your heart, and peace into your body. When you are at peace you are open to the flow of the life force in your body and in your life. When you are at peace you are open to receiving, which means you are open to receiving more of what you want to experience.

Being grateful opens your heart not only to joy and peace but also to love. Being grateful enables you to love. Being grateful is a path to love. Open your heart by being grateful.

Exercises: **Gratitude**

1. Think now of something or someone you love, and feel grateful for them in your life. Do you feel the opening, the warmth?

2. Keep a gratitude journal and give appreciation to yourself and those in your life and see how your life changes!

   Wisdom is more than intelligence. It is your insight, understanding and your ability to see from a larger perspective what you have learned from life's lessons. Through all the lessons and challenges, I finally got it. I turned within. I stopped looking outside myself for answers and guidance. Yes, there are teachers and guides to help us remember, but the truth is within us.

⟨∼SPIRITUAL PRINCIPLE∼⟩
Claim Your Wisdom and Power.

   Your wisdom and power are within you. The wisdom of God speaks directly to you in the form of your Spiritual Self through your intuition. The love that is within you is your **power**. Center into the love within you. You have the power to act; the power to express; the power to give your gifts to the world, your community, your family and yourself.

This is my life and these *Spiritual Principles and Practices* helped me to love myself more, know my purpose and live authentically. I learned how to claim my wisdom and power. This is your life. Choose it. Live your life with your heart open choosing love, choosing to be your authentic self. Do the work to clear yourself of limiting beliefs and emotional garbage.

Apply the *Spiritual Principles and Practices.* Life is too short to live not being your authentic self or not doing the things that fill your heart with joy. Stay grounded and centered in your Spirit.

~

Appendix

Spiritual Principles:

Definition of Therapeutic Touch

Therapeutic Touch is a healing modality, developed in the early 1970's by Delores Krieger, Ph.D. RN. professor at New York University and Dora Kunz, a natural healer. Therapeutic Touch is based on ancient healing practices using the laying on of hands and working with the electromagnetic vital energy field of the body which accelerates the body's own natural healing ability by opening up areas of congestion so energy can flow and balance. Healing is a return to wholeness and balance. It is a sense of well being.

Therapeutic Touch is a scientifically based healing practice. Experimental research has been conducted at major hospital centers and universities by scientists in nursing and related health care fields. The National Institute of Health has funded some of this research.